FISCAL INCIDENCE IN TIMOR-LESTE

IMPACT OF TAXATION AND PUBLIC EXPENDITURE ON POVERTY AND INEQUALITY

JULY 2024

ASIAN DEVELOPMENT BANK

© 2024 Asian Development Bank
6 ADB Avenue, Mandaluyong City, 1550 Metro Manila, Philippines
Tel +63 2 8632 4444; Fax +63 2 8636 2444
www.adb.org

Some rights reserved. Published in 2024.

ISBN 978-92-9270-595-4 (print); 978-92-9270-596-1 (electronic); 978-92-9270-597-8 (e-book)
Publication Stock No. SPR230620-2
DOI: http://dx.doi.org/10.22617/SPR230620-2

Notes:
1. This study was conducted under TA 9122-TIM: Timor-Leste, Fiscal Policy for Improved Service Delivery. This study was managed by David Freedman, former Country Economist, and the publication was managed by Kavita Iyengar, Economist, Southeast Asia Department.
2. In this publication, "$" refers to United States dollars.

On the cover: *Common folk and market scenes from Timor-Leste* (photos by Luis Enrique Ascui/ADB).

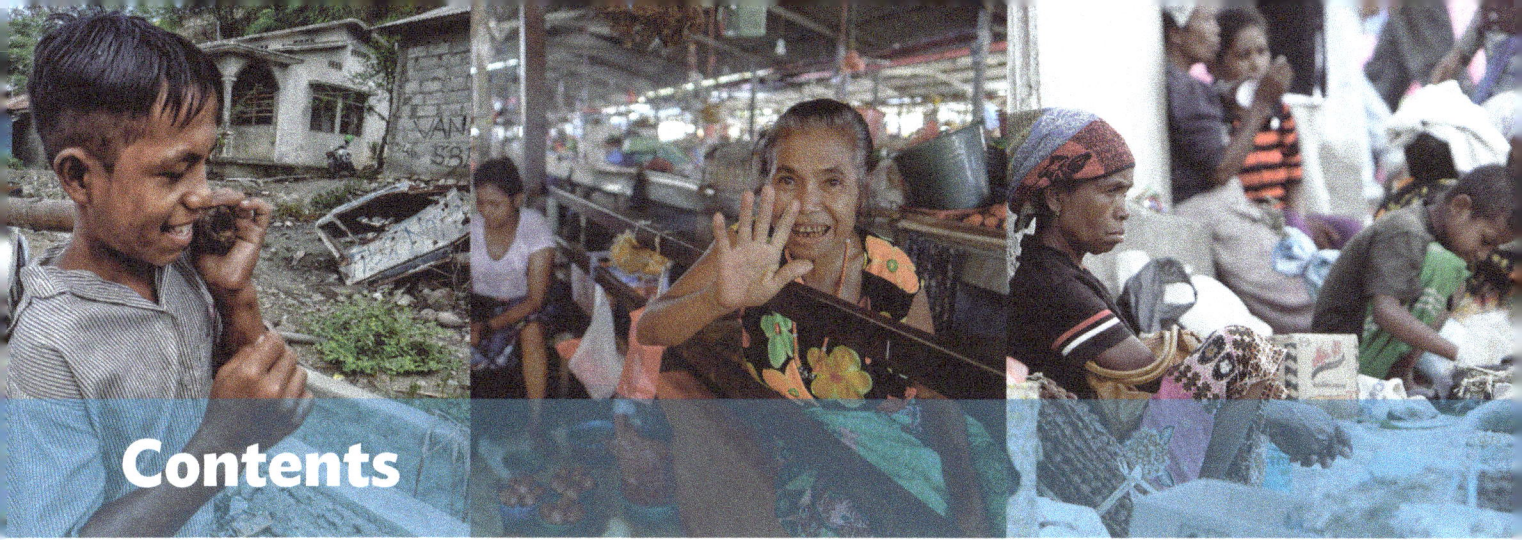

Contents

Tables and Figures

Foreword

Timor-Leste's experience provides an important example of how fiscal policies can support post-crisis recovery. Since 2006, successive governments have used the revenues from offshore oil and gas production to fund new social assistance programs, scale up spending on health and education, and upgrade infrastructure. These programs helped reduce the proportion of the population below the international poverty line of $1.90 per day from 47.2% in 2007 to 30.3% in 2014, the last year for which nationally representative survey data is available.

As part of its ongoing partnership with Timor-Leste's Ministry of Finance, the Asian Development Bank (ADB) has helped the Government of Timor-Leste to complete the first comprehensive fiscal incidence analysis for the country. The analysis, which is presented in this report, was prepared through a partnership with the Commitment to Equity (CEQ) Institute. The results of the analysis are striking, with Timor-Leste achieving one of the largest poverty reductions of any country where the CEQ framework has been applied.

The analysis shows cash and near-cash transfers reduced the poverty headcount by 10.4 percentage points which is further reduced by 11 percentage points when the estimated value of in-kind health and education services is added to households' income. The analysis also shows that fiscal policy is progressive in the sense that it serves to reduce inequality, with an estimated reduction in the Gini coefficient from 0.32 to 0.27. The reduction in inequality is small when compared to the magnitude of poverty reduction. However, cross-country analysis shows that the reduction in inequality seen in Timor-Leste is above average considering the country's level of development.

The expansion of programs benefiting households without any concurrent increase in households' tax burden may have supported Timor-Leste's social stability and peace-building process. However, over time, Timor-Leste is likely to face growing pressure to both increase domestic revenue mobilization and to adjust expenditures to maximize development impacts.

I would like to commend Epifanio Martins, National Director of Economic Policy, Ministry of Finance, Government of Timor-Leste, and the entire team for this excellent analysis. I would like to thank ADB for their support in the preparation of this timely and useful report.

Helder Lopes
Governor, Banco Central de Timor-Leste

Preface

Many countries in Asia and the Pacific continue to face unprecedented challenges in the wake of the coronavirus pandemic. Against this backdrop, fiscal policy has never been more important. Governments in the region have responded to the pandemic with new packages of tax relief, wage subsidies, and cash transfers. These measures have proven crucial in stemming the crisis. As governments transition from emergency response to economic recovery, they may face difficult choices about how to rebuild revenues and rationalize their future spending. Looking ahead, it will be important to ensure that fiscal policies remain consistent with growth and macroeconomic stability.

Changes in fiscal policies can have significant impacts on both poverty and income inequality. By analyzing the incidence of taxation and expenditures among different segments of the population, it is possible to obtain a clear picture of how fiscal policy impacts income distribution across society. This analysis can help governments better understand the overall impact of their current policies, and better evaluate different policy options.

Fiscal incidence analysis is a tool that can be used to support changes in fiscal policy. This report presents a series of policy simulations which consider the revenue and distributional impacts of possible changes in the design of expenditure programs or instruments for revenue collection in Timor-Leste. We hope the methodology, analysis, and results presented in this report will be insightful for stakeholders in Timor-Leste, and for other countries in Asia and the Pacific.

On behalf of the Asian Development Bank, I would like to express my appreciation for the excellent collaboration with the Government of Timor-Leste and Commitment to Equity Institute in delivering this study.

Winfried Wicklein
Director General
Southeast Asia Department
Asian Development Bank

Acknowledgments

The analysis drew on data provided by a range of Government of Timor-Leste agencies and development partners. This report was written by a team from Timor-Leste's Ministry of Finance and Commitment to Equity Institute. Stephen D. Younger led the team and was supported by Carlos Conde J.T. Neves de Camoes, Alzira Doutel, Maya Goldman, Francisco Soares de Jesus, Cirilo Pereira Mendonca, and Nilton Vicente. Overall guidance and supervision of the team was provided by Epifanio Martins, National Director of Economic Policy, Ministry of Finance, Government of Timor-Leste.

The team would like to acknowledge the contributions provided by the officials and advisors of the Government of Timor-Leste, as listed below.

Ministry of Planning and Finance. Fernanda Borges, Coordinator, Fiscal Reform Commission; Januario da Gama, General Director of State Finance; Elias dos Santos Ferreira, General Director of Statistics; Epifanio Martins, National Director of Economic Policy; Mónica Rangel da Cruz, General Director of Tax Authority; Cristino Gusmao, National Director of Economic Social Statistics; Silvino Lopes, National Director, System and Reports; Ostialina Dulce Anabela C.P. Santos, National Director of Revenue Accounting, Tax Authority; Uldarico Rodrigues, National Director of Declarative, Liquidation, and Collection Management, Tax Authority; M. da Costa Belo, Chief of Information System Unit, Tax Authority; Gerardo A. Puga, National Accounts, Non-Resident Advisor, General Directorate of Statistics.

Ministry of Agriculture. Faustino T.G. da Costa, National Director, National Directorate of Policy and Planning for Monitoring and Legal Matters; Carlos da Costa Lemos, Chief of Department, Department of Policy and Planning.

Ministry of Education. Antoninho Pires, General Director, Administration and Finance; Manuel Monteiro, National Director, Administration and Finance; Jose dos Santos, Chief of Department, Administration and Finance; Justino Varela, Chief of Department, Finance, Administration and Logistics; Rui Freitas, National Consultant, Finance.

Ministry of Health. Marcelo Amaral, National Director, Administration and Finance.

Ministry of Public Works, National Directorate of Electricity. Jose Smith, Chief of Department, National Directorate of Customer Support; Jose Fernandes, National Director, National Directorate of Customer Support.

Ministry of Social Solidarity. Aida Maria Soares Mota, National Director, National Directorate of Social Contribution Scheme; Lourenco Marques da Silva, National Directorate of Social Contribution Scheme; Nuno Gabriel Sá, Technical Advisor, National Directorate for the Combatants of National Liberation.

The team is grateful for the support of the following multilateral agencies.

International Labour Organization. André F. Bongestabs, Social Protection Officer.

World Bank. Adelaide Neves de Camoes, Education Specialist, Education Program; David Knight, Senior Economist, Macroeconomics Trade and Investment; Eric Vitale, Program Coordinator, Country Management Unit.

Executive Summary

This report presents the first comprehensive fiscal incidence analysis to be prepared for Timor-Leste. This analysis was carried out by applying the methodology developed by the Commitment to Equity (CEQ) Institute to data from the 2014 Timor-Leste Survey of Living Standards and a range of Government of Timor-Leste administrative sources.[1]

Using the CEQ framework enables the results from this analysis to be compared with other countries where the CEQ methodology has been applied. The analysis found that Timor-Leste's fiscal measures to support the nominal income of households had a positive impact on reducing the poverty rate. The overall impact on poverty reduction is larger than any other country where the CEQ methodology has been applied, with the exception of Georgia.

In 2014, which is the last year for which detailed household survey data is available, cash and near-cash transfers reduced the poverty headcount by 10.4 percentage points. When the estimated value of in-kind health and education services is added to households' income, then the poverty headcount falls by a further 11 percentage points. Taxes increase poverty, but by small amounts, reflecting the small tax take in Timor-Leste.

The impact of fiscal policy on income inequality is less dramatic. The analysis shows that fiscal policy is progressive in the sense that it serves to reduce inequality, with an estimated reduction in the Gini coefficient from 0.32 to 0.27. The reduction in inequality is small when compared to the magnitude of poverty reduction. However, cross country analysis shows that the reduction in inequality seen in Timor-Leste is above average considering the country's level of development.

These striking results reflect two broad features of Timor-Leste's development since independence. Firstly, inequality is low, and many households have incomes close to the national poverty line. Secondly, the government has used part of the income from offshore oil and gas production to finance several large social assistance programs and a significant increase in spending on education. To-date, financing of these programs has not required additional mobilization of domestic revenues, thus enabling an unusual situation in which representative households from all deciles of the income distribution are net beneficiaries of government services. This means that the value of transfer payments, subsidies, and in-kind services that households receive from government exceeds the payments they make to the government through direct and indirect taxes.

The expansion of programs benefiting households without any concurrent increase in households' tax burden may have supported Timor-Leste's social stability and peace-building process. However, it is unlikely to be sustainable in the long-term unless there are further large natural resource developments. Over time, Timor-Leste is likely to face growing pressure to both increase domestic revenue mobilization and to adjust expenditures to maximize development impacts. Fiscal incidence analysis is a tool that can be used to support changes in fiscal policy. To demonstrate this, the report presents a series of policy simulations which consider the revenue and

---

[1]   This empirical study is based on the dataset for household income, expenditure and consumption patterns, and national poverty line estimates in the *Poverty in Timor-Leste 2014* and *Timor-Leste Survey of Living Standards 2014* reports.

distributional impacts of possible changes in the design of expenditure programs or instruments for revenue collection.

The analysis finds that most poverty reduction is achieved through the old-age and veterans pensions. Neither of these social transfers are targeted on the basis of poverty. Timor-Leste's relatively flat and compressed income distribution made it difficult to develop proxy-mean tests for identifying poor households. This undermined efforts to design a conditional cash transfer for the targeted household segments. Hence, it is critical to make cash transfer programs better targeted based on the recent income distribution data and proxy-mean tests.[2] The report presents a number of simulations of changes in the design of this program, including establishment of a universal child benefit. The report also finds that when savings from phasing out electricity subsidies to the general population are redirected to the poor through social assistance programs such as *Bolsa da Mãe*, poverty and inequality decreases without any additional cost to the budget.

The analysis of direct and indirect taxes presented in the report shows that the incidence of these taxes is relatively progressive, and that small design changes can help to safeguard or reinforce this progressivity while also enabling greater revenue collection. This suggests that future efforts to increase domestic revenue collection through changes in the rates or thresholds for personal income tax or introduction of a value added tax will not necessarily lead to a significant increase in poverty. Indeed, such measures could be used to finance additional expenditures that are relatively concentrated among poor households, thus helping to achieve a net reduction in poverty and inequality without further undermining fiscal sustainability.

In considering the results presented in this report, it is important to be clear about some of the limitations of the analysis. Timor-Leste's economy has changed since 2014 and so the overall impact of different fiscal policy instruments will also have changed to some extent. Perhaps more importantly, there are some inherent limits in the scope for fiscal policy to directly drive poverty reduction. While it is necessary to look at how taxation and spending affects household incomes, it is equally pertinent to remain attentive to the ways in which public policies influence households' productive potential and the incentives that they face.

---

[2] Bolsa da Mãe – Jerasaun Foun, Technical Note#2-2021. *Bolsa da Mãe Jerasaun Foun is planned to be implemented as a universal program for the target population, i.e., pregnant women and early childhood.*

1. Introduction

One of the functions of a government is to redistribute resources, especially to the most disadvantaged members of society. Although there is considerable disagreement over both the extent and the means to effect such redistribution, most people agree that society is better off if inequality and poverty can be reduced, and all governments do, in fact, redistribute income with their tax and expenditure policies. The purpose of this report is to examine the extent to which the Government of Timor-Leste does so. In particular, the report addresses four general questions:

(i)   How much redistribution and income poverty reduction is being accomplished through revenue collection, social spending, and subsidies?

(ii) How progressive are revenue collection, subsidies, and government social spending?

(iii) How effective are revenue collection, subsidies, and government social spending at reducing inequality and poverty?

(iv) Within the limits of fiscal prudence, what could be done to increase redistribution and poverty reduction through changes in taxation and spending?

To put these questions in context, Timor-Leste is a very young country, having regained independence in 2002. At independence, it was also very poor, so the government's ability to tax and spend was quite limited. Those restrictions changed dramatically with the development of Bayu-Undan, an offshore oil and gasfield that came online in 2004. While all petroleum revenues are paid into a sovereign wealth fund—the Petroleum Fund—transfers from the fund to government were sufficient to allow government spending to more than double in real terms between 2008 and 2016 (World Bank, 2021).[1] While a large share of that spending went to much-needed infrastructure, the kinds of social spending that feature in an incidence analysis—education, health, and transfer payments—also increased substantially. Education spending per student more than doubled during the same period,[2] transfer payments increased by 50%,[3] and health spending per capita by approximately 30%,[4] all in real terms. Timor-Leste now has social spending shares that look more like a middle income country than a poor one, especially with regard to its transfer payments.

Has that extra spending paid off in terms of poverty and inequality reduction? The short answer is a resounding "yes" for poverty reduction, and "not much" for inequality. The analysis presented in this

---

[1]   Timor-Leste followed a duodecimal regime if the state budget was not passed by the Parliament. In such a case, one-twelfth of the previous year's budget was to be utilized monthly. This happened in 2017 and 2020. Public expenditure in 2021 was further impacted by the continuation of the COVID-19 pandemic and flooding due to cyclone Seroja. There was limited capital expenditure, but government expenditure remained persistently high with spending on public transfers, personal benefits transfers, and grants increasing significantly by 31% per annum during 2017–2021.

[2]   World Bank Data. Current Health Expenditure per Capita (current US$) – Timor-Leste. https://data.worldbank.org/indicator/SH.XPD.CHEX.PC.CD?end=2016&locations=TL&start=2009.

[3]   Transfer payments refer to cash payments made to households rather than transfers from central government to other public entities. | Government of Timor-Leste (2017).

[4]   World Health Organization (WHO). Global Health Expenditure Database. https://apps.who.int/nha/database/country_profile/Index/en.

report shows that Timor-Leste's combination of taxes and social spending lowers poverty more than any other country where the Commitment to Equity (CEQ) Institute has done an assessment except Georgia. But those same taxes and expenditures lower inequality very little. These results derive from three key features of Timor-Leste's government budget. First, as noted, social spending is relatively high and much of that spending is for cash transfers. This helps to reduce income poverty. But second, rather than going mostly to poor people, Timor-Leste's social spending is spread rather evenly across the population, so it does not reduce inequality as much as it could. And third, government taxes its population very little – less than 4% of gross national income (GNI).[5] Instead, it funds itself with petroleum revenues. So Timor-Leste's citizens get the benefits of public spending without the costs of taxation. This makes the poverty reduction effect of the budget especially strong, since taxes considered alone can only increase poverty.[6] But it also means that taxes have little effect on inequality.

Could Timor-Leste do better? Several specific policy simulations are considered in section 6, but the previous paragraph suggests a general conclusion: better targeting of social expenditures could improve the poverty and inequality reduction that the budget achieves. Unfortunately, it seems to be more difficult to target poor people in Timor-Leste than in other countries. The income distribution is both dense and flat around the poverty line, making it difficult to find indicators that separate poor people from near-poor people. Improved targeting will be a challenge and the cost effectiveness will need to be carefully evaluated.

Every incidence analysis should include a preemptory caution. When one tax or expenditure is found to be more redistributive to poor people than another, the temptation is to conclude that the former is preferable. But it is important to remember that redistribution is only one of many criteria that matter when making public policy. In particular, efficiency matters too, so not all redistributive taxes or expenditures are good ones, and not all good taxes or expenditures are redistributive. The results of this study and of all incidence studies are one input to public policymaking, one that should be weighed with other goals before deciding that a tax or expenditure is desirable.

---

[5]   Throughout the paper, GNI rather than gross domestic product (GDP) is used as a measure of available resources. In Timor-Leste, measurement of GDP has changed over time due to inclusion or exclusion of the value of off-shore oil and gas production. Gross national income has the advantage of integrating non-oil GDP and the income streams from offshore oil and gas production and Petroleum Fund investments which are available to finance public expenditures.

[6]   Indeed, in most countries with CEQ assessments, taxes, especially indirect taxes, increase poverty quite a lot, often enough to overwhelm the poverty-reducing effects of social spending.

2. Methods and Approach

The paper uses incidence analysis, a description of who benefits when the government spends money and who loses when the government taxes, following the methods developed by the CEQ Institute (Lustig, 2017).[1] Although it is possible to use incidence analysis to examine one particular expenditure or tax, the thrust of the assessment is rather to get a comprehensive picture of the redistributive effect of as many tax and expenditure items as possible. This is accomplished by comparing five core income concepts and their components. Figure 1 shows the relationship between these income measures and helps to illustrate how they may be used to analyze the distributional effects of fiscal policy.

Market income is income before the government has had any influence on the income distribution with its tax and spending policies. It includes all earned and unearned income except government transfers.[2] This is sometimes called "pre-fisc" income.

Disposable income is cash income available after the government has taken away direct taxes such as wage income tax and distributed direct transfers such as the *Bolsa da Mãe* and pensions, as well as "near cash" transfers such as free meals at school (*Merenda Eskolar*). Because direct taxes and transfers often have very different distributional consequences, it is helpful to consider their influence separately, thus the two intermediate income concepts between market and disposable income in Figure 1. Gross income is market income plus direct transfers; net market income is market income less direct taxes.

While that is the end of government's impact on nominal cash income, many government policies affect households' real income indirectly by altering the prices they pay for goods and services. Consumable income is disposable income less indirect taxes—sales tax, services tax, import duties, and excise taxes—plus indirect subsidies, such as the electricity that *Eletricidade de Timor-Leste* provides for free (in rural areas) or at rates well below cost (in Dili, and to government and firms). These indirect taxes and subsidies affect households' welfare by changing the prices they pay for goods and services.

The last way that a government influences the income distribution is through the provision of free or subsidized services such as health and education. Final income is consumable income plus the monetary value of these in-kind benefits, less any user fees paid for those services. Moving from consumable to final income highlights the effect on poverty and inequality of public health and education expenditures. Note that in Timor-Leste, the government supports both public and private schools, though the support for private schools is less per student (Appendix I). The study examines public and private school benefits separately.

The assessment compares standard indicators of inequality and poverty for each of the income concepts in Figure 1 to show how each aspect of the budget changes the distribution of income. In addition, it examines how specific individual line items affect inequality and poverty. Appendix II gives a brief explanation of the inequality and poverty indicators used.

---

1   For more details, visit www.commitmentoequity.org.
2   In addition, market income includes social insurance pensions if the recipient paid into the insurance scheme during their working years because these are considered deferred compensation rather than transfers. Until very recently, Timor-Leste had not had a contributory pension system, so pensions are best viewed as transfer payments here.

Figure 1   Definition of the Commitment to Equity Income Concepts

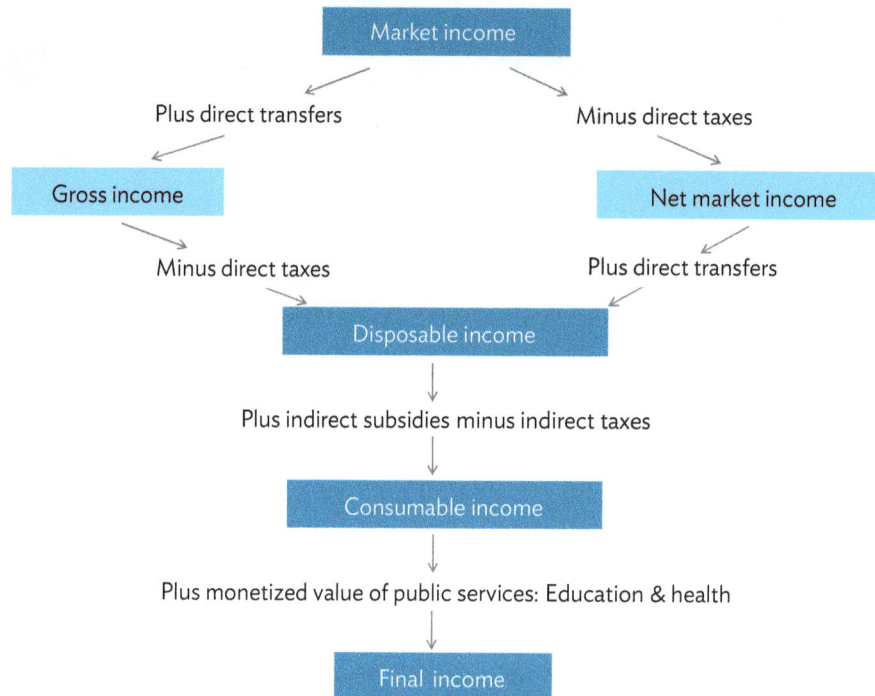

```
                            ┌─────────────────────┐
                            │    Market income    │
                            └─────────────────────┘
                          ↙                         ↘
         Plus direct transfers                        Minus direct taxes
              ↙                                                 ↘
  ┌─────────────────────┐                        ┌─────────────────────┐
  │    Gross income     │                        │   Net market income │
  └─────────────────────┘                        └─────────────────────┘
              ↘                                          ↙
        Minus direct taxes                     Plus direct transfers
                      ↘                          ↙
                    ┌─────────────────────────┐
                    │    Disposable income    │
                    └─────────────────────────┘
                                 ↓
              Plus indirect subsidies minus indirect taxes
                                 ↓
                    ┌─────────────────────────┐
                    │    Consumable income    │
                    └─────────────────────────┘
                                 ↓
         Plus monetized value of public services: Education & health
                                 ↓
                    ┌─────────────────────────┐
                    │      Final  income      │
                    └─────────────────────────┘
```

Source: Derived from Nora Lustig, and Sean Higgins. 2017. The CEQ Assessment: Measuring the Impact of Fiscal Policy on Inequality and Poverty. Chapter 1 in Nora Lustig, ed. *CEQ Handbook: Estimating the Impact of Fiscal Policy on Inequality and Poverty*. Brookings Institution. Washington, DC.

The assumptions with respect to the economic incidence of taxes are simple: direct taxes are borne entirely by the income earner; indirect taxes are borne entirely by the consumer. This latter assumption is not entirely appropriate if markets are not competitive, and many are not in Timor-Leste. However, the extent to which monopolies or oligopolies shift indirect taxes to consumers is not clear and could be either greater or less than 100%, depending on the functional form of the demand function (Fullerton and Metcalf, 1992).

Since there is no information on those functional forms, it is assumed that 100% of taxes are shifted to consumers regardless of market structure.

The one exception to these simple incidence assumptions is for a group of small programs which distribute a variety of agricultural inputs to farmers. For these programs, it is assumed that the benefits go to the food producers that receive them rather than to food consumers.

3. Data

Data Sources

To understand the distributional consequences of taxes and public expenditures, data on all of the above income concepts is needed for a representative sample of individuals in the country. This data is used to construct income distributions for each income concept outlined in the previous section and derive summary statistics for those distributions, as described in Appendix II. In Timor-Leste, the most recent such survey is the 2014/15 Timor-Leste Survey of Living Standards (TLSLS) (World Bank, 2016). In addition, administrative tax and expenditure data from the 2014 fiscal year is used to estimate some of the information needed, most specifically, the per beneficiary amount of spending on public education and health services.

Data Limitations

While an effort is made to include as many taxes and transfers as possible in the analysis, there are two limiting factors. First, many government expenditures are for genuine public goods like national defense (the military), public order (the police and courts), and policy development and implementation (the civil service). It is impossible to know how much these services are worth to any particular individual because unlike market goods and services, public goods do not have prices that people reveal themselves to be willing to pay. So large sections of government expenditure must be excluded from the analysis. Second, only those taxes and expenditures can be studied for which payers and beneficiaries can be identified in the TLSLS survey data. For example, who pays wage income tax can be inferred because the survey asks respondents about their wage earnings. But corporate income taxes cannot be attributed to survey respondents because there are no questions about corporate ownership. Table 1 lists all the tax and expenditure items included in the assessment. Appendix I gives detailed information about how information on each of these items was derived from the TLSLS data.

Overall, the assessment includes tax items accounting for 53% of total tax revenue, worth 2% of GNI and 25% of total expenditures, worth 9% of GNI. See Appendix I, Table A1.3 and Table A1.4 for details.

Table 1   Tax and Expenditure Items Included in the Assessment

Direct Taxes	Indirect Taxes
Wage income tax	Sales tax
Self-employment tax	Import duties
	Excise taxes
	• Petrol
	• Alcohol
	• Tobacco
	Services tax (telephone only)

Direct Transfers	Indirect Transfers
Bolsa da Mãe	Electricity subsidy
Retirement pension	
Disability pension	
Combatants' and martyrs' pension	
School Meals	
Housing reconstruction and repair	
Miscellaneous others	

In-kind Schooling Benefits	In-kind Health Benefits
Pre-primary	Inpatient care
Basic school	Outpatient care
Secondary school	• at hospitals
Post-secondary school	• at district health centers and posts
	• at mobile clinics

Note: The *Bolsa da Mãe* (Mother's Purse) is a conditional cash transfer program for mothers of children under 17 years old. It pays $5 per child per month for up to three children.

Construction of the Income and Expenditure Variables

A detailed description of how each element of the CEQ income and expenditure variables is calculated can be found in Appendix 1. The Stata "do-files" (programs) used to generate these variables are also available on request.

Disposable Income
Construction of the CEQ income concepts starts with disposable income and works backward to market incomes and forward to final incomes (Figure 1). It is assumed that the welfare measure most commonly used from the TLSLS—household expenditure—is conceptually closest to disposable income. The expenditure variable as constructed by the General Directorate of Statistics is used. There are theoretical arguments as to why a household's expenditure may best reflect its permanent income, but the motivation is mostly practical: in countries with a high degree of informal and self-employment, surveys like the TLSLS measure expenditures more accurately than they measure incomes. To use this starting point, it is assumed that household net savings are zero, that is, disposable income is exactly equal to measured household expenditure.[1]

Market Income, Net Market Income, and Gross Income
Market income is constructed by adding the direct taxes listed in Table 1—wage income tax and taxes on the self-employed—to disposable income and subtracting all of the direct transfers—the *Bolsa da*

Mãe; pensions for retirees, people with disabilities, and veterans; school meals; reconstruction assistance for victims of disasters triggered by natural hazards; and miscellaneous other items. Gross income and net market income follow directly, as shown in Figure 1.

Consumable Income

Consumable income is calculated adding indirect subsidies to disposable income and subtracting indirect taxes paid. The assessment includes only one indirect subsidy, for electricity, and all the main indirect taxes—sales tax, import duties, services tax (on telephone service only)—and excises on petroleum products, alcohol, and tobacco.

Final Income

Households' final income is calculated by adding in-kind transfers associated with public provision of education and health care to consumable income. The benefit associated with schooling by school level (pre-school, basic school, secondary school, and post-secondary school) and ownership/management (public or private) is estimated.[2] The latter do receive support from the government, albeit less than the public schools. For publicly provided health care, inpatient stays and outpatient care at hospitals, district health facilities, and mobile clinics may be identified.

---

[2]   Basic schools (*eskolabasiku*) combine primary school, grades 1–6, with lower secondary, grades 7–9.

4. Results

There are many measures of poverty and inequality, but the most common by far are the income poverty headcount—the share of the population with income below the poverty line—and the Gini coefficient. The "poverty gap" measures the average percentage shortfall of poor people's income compared to the poverty line (Appendix II).

Impact of Taxes and Social Expenditures on Poverty and Inequality

Table 2 shows the Gini coefficient, the poverty headcount, and the poverty gap for the CEQ income variables. These allow us to assess the general impact of taxes and social expenditures on the income distribution.

The Gini coefficient shows statistically significant drops at two points: between net market income and gross income, and between consumable income and

Table 2 Inequality and Poverty for Commitment to Equity Income Measures

	Gini	Headcount	Poverty Gap
Market income	0.320	0.517	0.168
Net market income	0.319	0.520	0.169
Gross income	0.289	0.413	0.103
Disposable income	0.288	0.415	0.103
Consumable income	0.286	0.409	0.100
Final income	0.270	0.299	0.062

Note: Poverty measured using the 2014 national poverty line of $556.5 per person per year.

Source: Timor-Leste Survey of Living Standards 2014/15 and authors' calculations.

final income. Recalling the construction of each income variable, this leads to four conclusions:

(i) Direct taxes have very little impact on inequality (compare market with net market income to see this). This is not because direct taxes are not progressive—rather, they collect small amounts of money (see Table A1.3) and so have little impact.

(ii) Cash and near-cash transfers—*Bolsa da Mãe*, pensions for veterans, retirement, and disability, free school meals, and other ad hoc assistance to households—reduce inequality by 3.1 percentage points. (Compare market income to gross income.) This is to be expected since many of these items are intended to benefit poorer households.

(iii) Indirect taxes and subsidies have almost no effect on inequality. (Compare disposable income to consumable income.) This is because they tend to be distributionally neutral, and because indirect taxes are also small shares of total revenue.

(iv) In-kind benefits of public spending on health and education reduce inequality by 1.6 percentage points. (Compare consumable income to final income.)

For perspective, the average reduction in the Gini coefficient from market income to final income in 31 countries where CEQ data available is 8.3 percentage points whereas this reduction in Timor-Leste is 5 percentage points (Figure 2). This reduction tends to be larger for higher income countries. Based on a regression of the change in the Gini coefficient on GDP per capita at purchasing power parity for the 31 countries mentioned, Timor-Leste's change is actually 2 percentage points better than one would predict based on its GDP per capita.

Figure 2   Change in Gini Coefficient from Market to Final Income

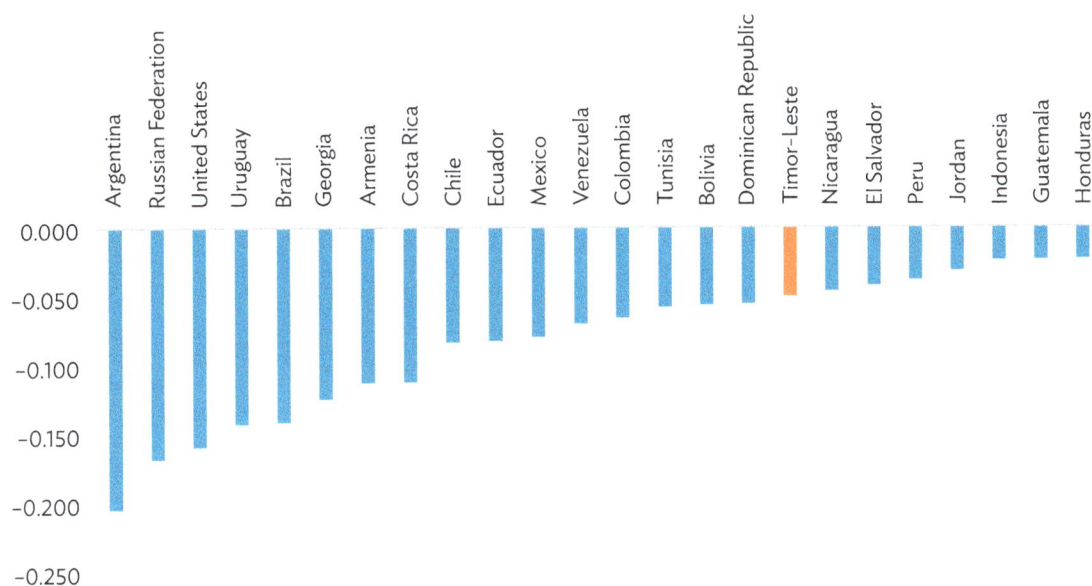

Note: All comparisons treat pensions as government transfers.

Source: Commitment to Equity. 2017. CEQ Standard Indicators. http://www.commitmentoequity.org/datacenter.

The effect of taxes and social expenditures on poverty shows a qualitatively similar but much more pronounced pattern across the CEQ income variables. Cash and near-cash transfers reduce the poverty headcount by 10.4 percentage points (compare market income with gross income); and in-kind health and education benefits lower poverty by 11 percentage points (compare consumable income to final income). Taxes, either direct or indirect, increase poverty, but by small amounts, reflecting the small tax take in Timor-Leste. This is unusual compared to other countries, especially for indirect taxes which tend to increase poverty by much more than observed here. This is partly due to the low amount of taxes collected and also to the offsetting effect of the indirect subsidy on electricity. Overall, taxes and expenditures have a very large effect on poverty, reducing the headcount by 21.8 percentage points. This is much larger than in other countries with CEQ assessments. The average decline from market income to consumable income[1] for 31 countries is 3.2 percentage points, compared to 10.8 percentage points in Timor-Leste. Further,

as with inequality, it is usually the case that the improvement increases with GDP per capita. Based on a regression across the 31 countries, no improvement in poverty may be expected for a country with Timor-Leste's GDP per capita (Figure 3).

Overall, then, Timor-Leste does well on both poverty and inequality reduction compared to other developing countries. This is neither due to especially effective targeting of social expenditures nor comparatively large social expenditures. Rather, Timor-Leste has much lower tax revenue than other countries and somewhat higher transfer payments. Direct taxes are 1.6% of GNI compared to an average of 6.1% in the other CEQ countries. Indirect taxes are 2.1% of GNI compared to 10%. Distributing a "normal" share of GNI in social expenditures while taxing relatively little improves the poverty numbers since tax can only increase poverty while benefits reduce it. It also tends to improve the change in inequality since taxes, especially indirect taxes, tend to be closer to neutral while expenditures are more progressive.

---

[1]   CEQ does not usually consider the poverty reducing impact of health and education expenditures because of concerns about the quality of the data used to value these benefits.

Figure 3   Change in Poverty Headcount from Market to Consumable Income

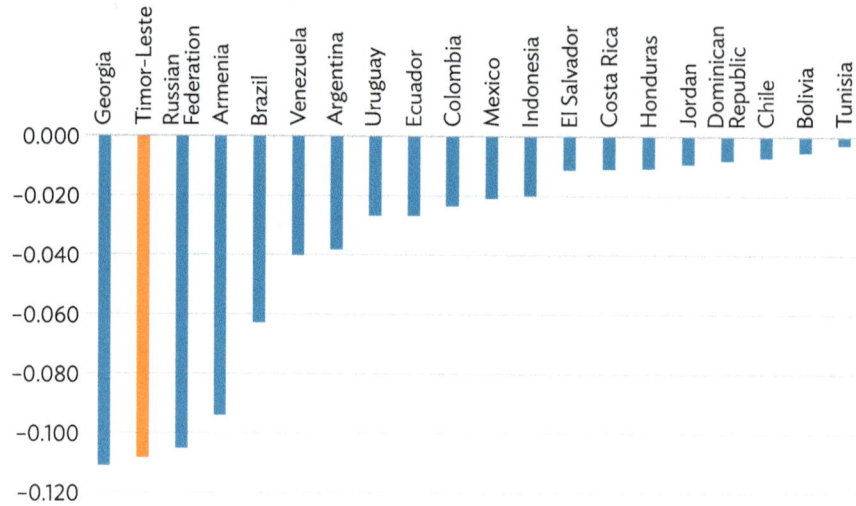

Note: All comparisons treat pensions as government transfers.

Source: Commitment to Equity. 2017. CEQ Standard Indicators. http://www.commitmentoequity.org/datacenter.

Figure 4 gives some perspective on this. It shows the net benefits for each decile of the income distribution broken down by the main tax and expenditure groups included in the study. There are two striking things about Figure 4. First, those in the poorest decile of the market income distribution get huge net benefits

Figure 4   Net Payers or Beneficiaries of Taxes and Social Expenditures by Decile

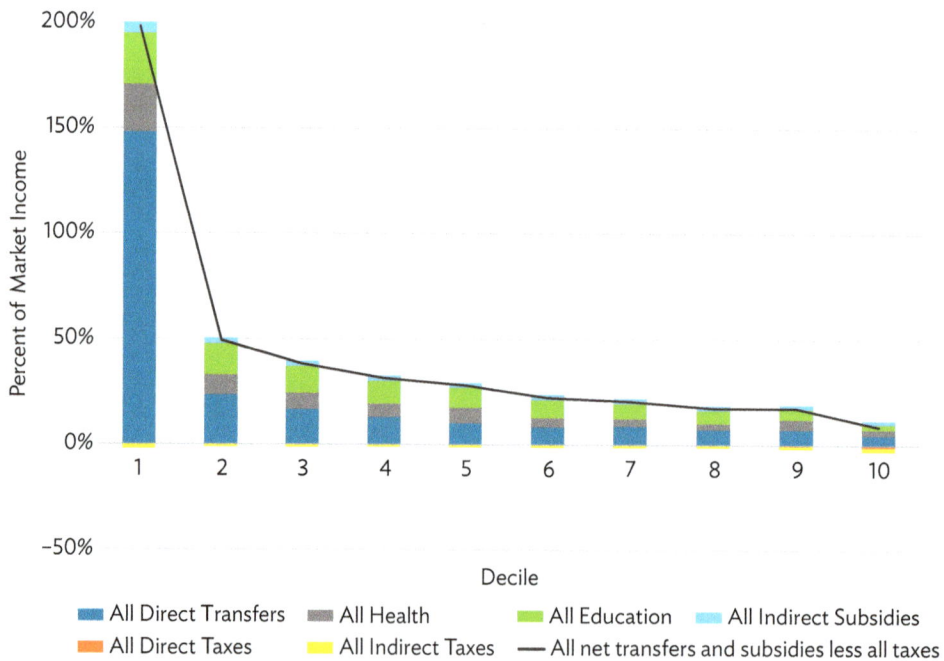

Source: Timor-Leste Survey of Living Standards 2014/15 and authors' calculations.

from the budget (almost 200% of their pre-tax income). This is mostly due to very large benefits from transfers—148% of their pre-tax income. Less obvious but still quite unusual is that every decile, even the richest, is a net beneficiary. Figure 5 makes this clearer by limiting the vertical axis at 50% of pre-fisc income. In most countries, households above the second or third deciles are net *payers*. Note, too, that even in the top decile, transfer payment receipts alone are almost as large as all tax payments, again, a highly unusual result. Such government expenditures are only made possible by the transfer of oil and gas revenue, which is not sustainable (Table A1.3).

Targeting the Incidence of Taxes and Expenditures

There are many ways to measure the targeting of taxes and expenditures. Table 3 presents three of these: concentration coefficients, marginal effects for the Gini coefficient (inequality), and marginal effects for the poverty headcount.[2]

Concentration coefficients are similar to Gini coefficients: they show how concentrated a tax or expenditure is among either poor or rich people. However, while Gini coefficients range from zero (income is spread evenly across the population) to

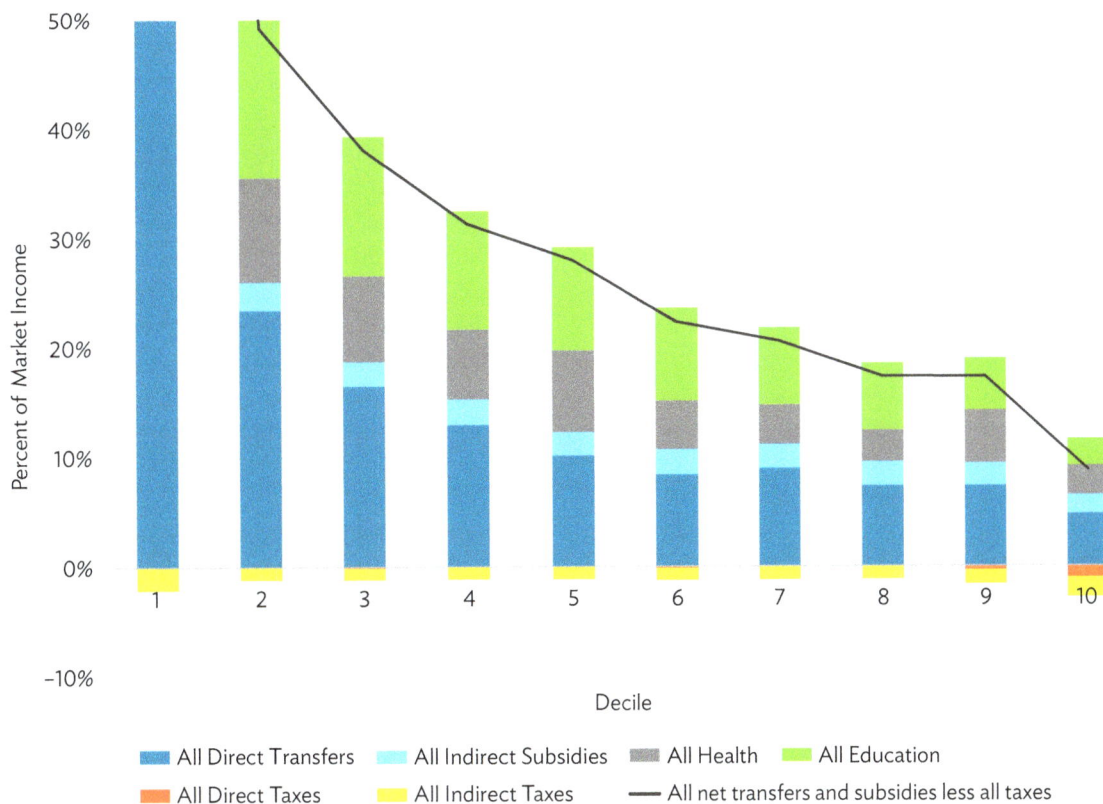

Figure 5   Net Payers or Beneficiaries of Taxes and Social Expenditures by Decile (Vertical Axis Truncated)

Legend:
- All Direct Transfers
- All Indirect Subsidies
- All Health
- All Education
- All Direct Taxes
- All Indirect Taxes
- All net transfers and subsidies less all taxes

Source: Timor-Leste Survey of Living Standards 2014/15 and authors' calculations.

---

[2]   See Appendix II for a detailed presentation of these measures, and Enami (2017) for a full discussion of other incidence measures.

one (income is completely concentrated among the richest people), concentration coefficients range from −1 to 1. A value of −1 indicates that all the tax or expenditure falls only on the poorest person; a value of 0 indicates that a tax or expenditure is spread evenly across the population; and a value of 1 indicates that a tax or expenditure falls only on the richest person. It is sometimes useful to compare the concentration coefficient to the Gini coefficient, given at the bottom of Table 3.[3] Taxes are considered to be "progressive" if they have a concentration coefficient greater than the Gini coefficient, i.e., they are more concentrated among rich people than is income. Expenditures are considered to be "progressive" only if the concentration coefficient is less than zero.[4]

Concentration coefficients show how the *shares* of a tax or expenditure are distributed across the population. As such, they do not change with program size: if the tax that everyone pays is doubled, the shares will not change and neither will the concentration coefficient. But for a large impact on overall poverty or inequality, the size of the tax or expenditure also matters. The two marginal effects measures take into account both the targeting and the size of a tax or expenditure. The marginal effect for the Gini coefficient is: [(Gini coefficient for market income) minus (Gini coefficient for market income plus/minus the expenditure or tax under consideration)] multiplied by 100. That is, it is the change in the market income Gini-induced by this one tax or expenditure alone. The marginal effect for the poverty headcount is defined similarly. Note that these definitions imply that a positive marginal effect shows a *reduction* in inequality or poverty.

Table 3 also includes a measure of spending "effectiveness." This is the ratio of the change in the absolute poverty gap[5] caused by the tax or expenditure divided by the total revenue or expenditure. If this measure is zero, it means that all its benefits go to nonpoor people. If it is one, it means that all its benefits go to people who are poor both before *and*

after the expenditure's benefits are considered. That is, all the expenditure serves to lower the poverty gap. In general, the measure gives the share of the expenditure that goes toward reducing the poverty gap. For a tax, on the other hand, the effectiveness measure shows what share of the tax revenue contributes to *increasing* the poverty gap. As such, for a tax, a value close to zero is "good" since it means that almost all of the revenue is collected from those who are not poor either before or after the tax is imposed.

Direct and Indirect Transfers

Direct and indirect transfers have a substantial effect on poverty and more limited effect on inequality. On average, veterans' pensions are the largest payment households receive from the government, accounting for 5.2% of pre-fisc income (market income). The number of beneficiaries of the veterans' pension has substantially increased over the years and possibly the coverage remains skewed toward the better off recipients, thus explaining the error of inclusion in the payment of the veteran's pension. The TLSLS 2014 estimated that the veterans' pension may have financed up to 47% of average Timor-Leste's household expenditures and 60% of the average household expenditures of the bottom 20%. Veterans' pensions are thus estimated to reduce poverty by 3.6 percentage points and inequality by 1.6 percentage points, more than any other item in the study. In part, this reflects their large budget, but these transfers are also among the most effective in terms of reducing the poverty gap. Given that veterans' pensions are much larger per recipient than other pensions, and large enough to push many recipients well above the poverty line, this seems a counterintuitive result. The explanation is that households receiving veterans' pensions often have little or no other income—their market income is close to zero. So based on market income, veterans' pension recipients are quite poor. Even if their pension pushes them over the poverty line, a large part of the pension serves to eliminate a poor recipient's poverty gap.

---

[3]   Indeed, another measure, the Kakwani coefficient, is the difference between these two.

[4]   This is sometimes termed as "pro-poor" and expenditures with concentration coefficients between zero and the Gini coefficient called "progressive."

[5]   The absolute poverty gap is the weighted sum of the difference between the poverty line and poor people's income. As such, it is measured in dollars.

Table 3   Targeting and Effectiveness of Social Expenditures

Expenditure	Size (Share of Market Income)	Concentration Coefficient	Marginal Effect, Gini	Marginal Effect, Poverty Headcount	Spending Effectiveness, Poverty Gap
Direct transfers	0.128	−0.228	3.09	10.43	0.437
Veterans' pension	0.052	−0.567	1.64	3.55	0.499
Bolsa da Mãe	0.006	−0.095	0.22	0.43	0.563
Retirement pension	0.038	0.054	0.56	3.32	0.388
Disability pension	0.005	0.155	0.04	0.36	0.335
Other cash transfers from government	0.005	−0.006	0.07	0.22	0.392
Free school meals	0.018	−0.064	0.67	1.77	0.551
Free tractor (use value)	0.002	0.063	0.05	0.06	0.486
Free motor (use value)	0.000	0.078	0.00	0.00	0.342
Miscellaneous agricultural inputs	0.000	−0.322	0.01	0.00	0.668
Free mosquito nets and repairs	0.000	0.011	0.01	0.02	0.511
Assistance to rebuild housing	0.001	−0.560	0.07	0.14	0.698
Free rice, maize, and other food	0.000	−0.170	0.01	0.00	0.589
Indirect subsidies	0.022	0.219	0.19	1.87	0.340
Electricity subsidy	0.022	0.219	0.19	1.87	0.340
In-kind benefits	0.123	−0.001	2.12	11.39	0.376
Publicly funded schooling	0.072	−0.017	2.10	7.53	0.475
Pre-primary in-kind benefits, public	0.001	0.080	0.02	0.05	0.469
Pre-primary in-kind benefits, private	0.000	0.394	0.00	0.06	0.121
Basic school in-kind benefits, public	0.055	−0.090	2.00	5.82	0.533
Basic school in-kind benefits, private	0.003	0.124	0.05	0.16	0.021
Secondary in-kind benefits, public	0.006	0.093	0.12	0.60	0.443
Secondary in-kind benefits, private	0.002	0.341	−0.01	0.21	0.089
Post-secondary in-kind benefits, public	0.003	0.373	−0.04	0.28	0.205
Post-secondary in-kind benefits, private	0.001	0.396	−0.01	0.06	0.096
Publicly funded health care	0.034	0.027	0.46	3.55	0.382
Inpatient care	0.013	0.031	−0.04	1.15	0.279
Outpatient care at hospital	0.006	−0.046	0.16	0.68	0.505
Outpatient care at district health facility	0.015	0.056	0.34	1.51	0.449
Outpatient care at mobile clinic	0.000	0.016	0.01	0.03	0.505
Headcount poverty for market income			0.517		
Gini coefficient for market income			0.320		

Notes:
1.   Concentration coefficients calculated on market income.
2.   Marginal effects are defined so that reductions in inequality or poverty have positive values.
3.   Marginal effects are multiplied by 100, so 1.0 is a 1 percentage point change.
4.   Size is measured with survey data; ratios can differ from administrative data. See Tables A1.3 and A1.4.
5.   All expenditures listed in 2014 continue to be in existence except "Free mosquito nets and repairs" and "Free rice, maize and other food".

Source: Timor-Leste Survey of Living Standards 2014/15 and authors' calculations.

Retirement pensions are the only transfer payment with a budget comparable to that for veterans' pensions—3.8% of market income. The concentration coefficient of 0.054 indicates that these pensions are spread almost evenly over the population. Retirement pensions' impact on the poverty headcount is substantial, almost as large as that for veterans' pensions, though their effect on inequality is much smaller. Retirement pensions' poverty gap effectiveness is also significantly less than that for veterans' pensions, another surprising result. Recipients of retirement pensions are more likely to be just below the poverty line before receiving their pension, which means their pension helps push them over the line and reduce the headcount. But retirement pensions' effect on the poverty gap is less than that for veterans' pensions because fewer retirement beneficiaries remain poor after receiving the transfer, so some of it is "wasted" by pushing them beyond the poverty line.

Disability pensions pay the same amount as retirement pensions, but to many fewer recipients. Their share of market income is only 0.5%. They are somewhat more concentrated among better-off households than retirement pensions, indicating that households that include a person with disabilities are not as poor as those with a retiree.

The *Bolsa da Mãe* is a much smaller transfer, one-tenth the amount of veterans' pensions, but it is intentionally targeted to poor people. Its concentration coefficient of −0.1 suggests that this targeting is only moderately successful. The *Bolsa da Mãe* is going disproportionately to poor households, but is less well-targeted than in most other countries (Figure 6). Nevertheless, its impact on poverty and inequality is about proportionate to veterans' pensions, reducing them by 0.43 and 0.22 percentage points, respectively. The poverty gap effectiveness for *Bolsa da Mãe* is a little better than veterans' pensions. It is also interesting to compare the *Bolsa da Mãe* with retirement pensions. The latter are less effective than the *Bolsa da Mãe*, but still have larger marginal effects because the budget for retirement pensions is much larger.

The only near-cash transfer that has a significant budget is free school meals for students in pre-school and primary school. These benefits amount to 1.8% of household market income, on average. This benefit has a concentration coefficient similar to the *Bolsa da Mãe* even though it is not means tested, and it has a large impact on both inequality and poverty relative to its size. Its poverty gap effectiveness is among the best of the transfers examined here.

The other near-cash transfers have small budgets and, therefore, only limited effects on poverty and inequality. It is worth noting that assistance with construction materials is extremely well-targeted to poor people and very effective at reducing the poverty gap. This may reflect the fact that these benefits are usually provided to the victims of disasters triggered by natural hazards. While it may not be reasonable to expand such a program significantly, it certainly is an effective approach to acute poverty alleviation.

Indirect Subsidies and In-Kind Benefits

The only indirect subsidy included in the assessment is the one for electricity. This is a very large budget item, accounting for 2.4% of households' market income. The subsidy has a concentration coefficient of 0.22, not well-targeted at poor people, but it nevertheless has a large effect on poverty, reducing it by 2.07 percentage points. This reflects the large size of the subsidy and also that many beneficiaries are just below the poverty line, as opposed to the poorest people who often do not have a connection to the electricity mains. Despite its large effect on headcount poverty, this subsidy is less effective at reducing the poverty gap than many of the transfers considered in the study.

The benefits of public schooling have a fairly typical pattern. Basic school has a small negative concentration coefficient, indicating that its benefits are spread fairly evenly across the population, but slightly more to poor people. This reflects the fact that households with school-age children tend to be slightly poorer on a per capita basis than other households and also that better-off households sometimes send their children to private schools as shown by the higher concentration curve for the benefits of private schooling. Pre-primary schooling is slightly more concentrated among better-off households because not all children, especially in poorer households, attend this level. The benefits of secondary and post-secondary education are more concentrated among rich people than basic school, but compared to other countries, the difference is not too great. Post-secondary education, in particular, has a lower concentration coefficient than in many other countries. The benefits that the government provides through its support to private schools are more concentrated among richer households than the benefits of public schools except at the university level where they are very similar.

The benefits from public basic schools as a share of household market income are at an order of magnitude larger than the other levels. This is where most students are enrolled. As such, basic school also has the largest inequality and poverty reducing effects of any item in the study. Its poverty gap effectiveness is also among the highest.

Health care, both inpatient and outpatient of all types, is spread remarkably evenly across the population which suggests that health care is available to all in Timor-Leste. The marginal effects on inequality are small, but all public health care reduces poverty by 3.5 percentage points, with the impact distributed across inpatient care, outpatient care at hospitals, and outpatient care at district health facilities in roughly the same proportions as expenditures on those services. But the poverty gap effectiveness of outpatient spending is significantly better than that for inpatient care.

Taxes

The direct taxes that can be observed in the TLSLS are highly concentrated among the richest households in the country (Table 4). This is due to the fact that (i) they are collected only from workers in the formal sector, who tend to be better off, and (ii) both income taxes on the self-employed and wage income tax are collected only on incomes over $500 per month.

Table 4   Targeting and Effectiveness of Taxes

Tax	Size (as a Share of Market Income)	Concentration Coefficient	Marginal Effect, Gini	Marginal Effect, Poverty Headcount	Spending Effectiveness, Poverty Gap
Direct taxes	−0.004	0.795	0.13	−0.25	−0.093
Wage income tax	−0.003	0.778	0.11	−0.25	−0.106
Personal income tax, self-employed	0.000	0.906	0.02	0.00	−0.007
Personal income tax, self-reported	0.000	0.905	0.01	0.00	−0.004
Indirect taxes	−0.013	0.380	0.07	−0.77	−0.275
Sales tax	−0.002	0.284	−0.01	−0.10	−0.326
Import duties	−0.002	0.284	−0.01	−0.09	−0.326
Services tax (phone only)	−0.001	0.343	0.00	−0.05	−0.263
Excises					
Petrol excise	−0.001	0.484	0.02	0.00	−0.196
Tobacco excise	−0.004	0.169	−0.07	−0.35	−0.396
Beer excise	−0.003	0.765	0.11	−0.07	−0.059
Wine excise	0.000	0.474	0.00	0.00	−0.190
Spirits excise	−0.001	0.838	0.03	0.00	−0.066
Headcount poverty for market income			0.517		
Gini coefficient for market income			0.320		

Source: Timor-Leste Survey of Living Standards 2014/15 and authors' calculations.

The progressivity of indirect taxes is more mixed. The larger indirect taxes, sales tax, and import duties are distributed similarly to market income. As such, they have very little impact on inequality (with the marginal effect being near zero) but they do increase poverty, about a percentage point each. Excise taxes on petrol are mildly progressive, though this does not include the indirect effect of these taxes on other goods and services. Excise taxes on beer and spirits are highly progressive. Tobacco excises, on the other hand, are regressive, a typical result. This does present a dilemma for policymakers who would like to discourage smoking by taxing tobacco more heavily. This may improve public health, but the tax will fall more heavily on poorer households. There is no such dilemma for alcohol taxation. All of the excises collect small amounts of revenue and thus, have small marginal effects on inequality and poverty. Many of the indirect taxes are less "effective" than direct taxes, but the excises on beer and spirits are exceptions. Poor people pay only very small shares of these taxes.

Coverage

Coverage is the number of people who receive a benefit divided by the total relevant population. Even when reported by quintile, as done here, coverage is a different measurement from concentration. A benefit that went only to the poorest person in the country would have an excellent concentration coefficient (–1), but very low coverage. On the other hand, benefits that have universal coverage have concentration coefficients close to zero. For some benefits like access to schooling or health care, good coverage is more important than a high concentration among poor people.

Table 5 gives coverage for transfer payments in Timor-Leste by quintile of market income. Over the entire population, relatively few people receive any transfer payment except retirement pensions, which is to be expected. It is rather striking that coverage for *Bolsa da Mãe* recipients is so even across the quintiles since this should be targeted to poor people. Almost all

Table 5   Coverage of Transfer Payments

Quintile	1	2	3	4	5	All
As a percentage of overall population						
Bolsa da Mãe	5	5	5	4	3	**4**
Retirement pension	7	5	6	6	9	**7**
Disability pension	1	1	1	1	2	**1**
Veteran's pension	4	1	0	1	1	**1**
Other cash transfer	1	0	0	1	1	**1**
As a percentage of 60 years plus population						
Retirement pension	75	74	76	77	75	**75**
Veteran's pension	40	11	4	7	4	**14**
As a percentage of all adults with disabilities						
Disability pension	24	37	30	37	48	**35**
Veteran's pension	134	37	10	27	17	**46**

Note: Quintiles are for market income. "1" is the poorest fifth of the population; "5" is the richest.

Source: Timor-Leste Survey of Living Standards 2014/15 and authors' calculations.

Table 6   Education Coverage

Quintile	1	2	3	4	5	All
As a percentage of all 6–11-year-olds						
Pre-school, public	1	2	1	2	3	**2**
Basic school, public	63	69	67	69	64	**66**
Pre-school, private	0	0	1	0	0	**0**
Basic school, private	8	7	10	11	14	**10**
Any schooling	73	78	80	83	82	**79**
As a percentage of all 12–14-year-olds						
Basic school, public	84	84	84	80	73	**81**
Secondary school, public	0	1	1	0	0	**0**
Basic school, private	9	9	12	15	23	**13**
Secondary school, private	0	0	0	0	1	**0**
Any schooling	93	94	96	96	97	**95**
As a percentage of all 15–17-year-olds						
Basic school, public	62	66	60	55	43	**57**
Secondary school, public	7	8	10	17	16	**11**
Tertiary, public	0	1	0	0	0	**0**
Basic school, private	7	7	12	12	19	**11**
Secondary school, private	4	3	2	4	10	**4**
Tertiary, private	0	0	1	0	1	**0**
Any schooling	80	84	84	88	89	**85**
As a percentage of all 18–21-year-olds						
Basic school, public	3	2	2	2	0	**2**
Secondary school, public	3	4	4	6	3	**4**
Tertiary, public	1	1	2	3	5	**2**
Basic school, private	0	0	0	0	0	**0**
Secondary school, private	0	0	3	1	2	**1**
Tertiary, private	1	3	6	6	10	**5**
Any schooling	8	11	17	18	21	**15**
As a percentage of all 22–25-year-olds						
Basic school, public	36	25	21	15	18	**23**
Secondary school, public	33	28	31	29	36	**31**
Tertiary, public	1	1	2	7	3	**3**
Basic school, private	3	2	4	5	4	**4**
Secondary school, private	4	5	12	8	15	**9**
Tertiary, private	2	2	4	6	7	**4**
Any schooling	78	63	74	71	83	**74**

Source: Timor-Leste Survey of Living Standards 2014/15 and authors' calculations.

elderly people receive either a retirement pension or a veterans' pension and the coverage is better in the lower quintiles than the top ones. Coverage is lower for persons with disabilities, though it is still quite good for the lower two quintiles.[6] It is striking how many people with disabilities receive a veterans' pension, especially in the lowest quintile, where there is clearly some overlap with receipt of a disability pension.

Table 6 gives coverage rates for schooling, both public and private, by age group and quintile. Coverage through age 17, when a student should finish secondary school, is high, though many students are at a lower grade than is appropriate for their age. Coverage in the poorer quintiles at these ages is lower than in the richer ones, but not by much. It is interesting that the share of students in private schools does not rise across the quintiles by as much as one might expect. This is due to classification of religious schools, some of which explicitly target poorer students, as private schools.

Coverage drops dramatically from primary school to secondary school but the decline is spread evenly over the quintiles. There is a huge difference between the 18–21-year-old cohort, which is largely out of school, and the 22–25-year-old cohort, which has much higher attendance. This may reflect differences in school entry around the time of independence. Just after independence, 18–21-year-olds would have been of age to enter school, while the older cohort should have entered just before. If the older cohort's entry was delayed because of low coverage before independence, that cohort may not have completed (or even started) its schooling. Timor-Leste has instituted an adult education program which may account for the high enrollment of 22–25-year-olds in both basic and secondary schools as the pre-independence cohorts catch up on their schooling.

Table 7 gives coverage for health care at different types of facilities. It is difficult to judge if this level of coverage is adequate. Clearly, not everyone would visit a health-care facility in a given month (the recall period in the TLSLS questionnaire). But it is encouraging that coverage for outpatient care is similar across the quintiles. Inpatient care, though, is twice as common in the highest quintile than the lowest.

Table 7   Health Care Coverage as a Percentage of Total Population in Quintile

Quintile	1	2	3	4	5	All
Inpatient care	0.7	0.6	0.9	0.6	1.4	**0.8**
Outpatient care by type of facility						
Hospital	1	3	2	2	2	**2**
District facility	9	8	10	10	12	**10**
Mobile clinic	0	0	1	0	0	**0**

Source: Timor-Leste Survey of Living Standards 2014/15 and authors' calculations.

---

[6]   Disability in the TLSLS is self-reported. There is no reason to believe that this is completely consistent with the government's criteria for receiving a disability pension. Coverage is greater than 100% for the first quintile because more people report receiving a veteran's pension than report being disabled in that quintile.

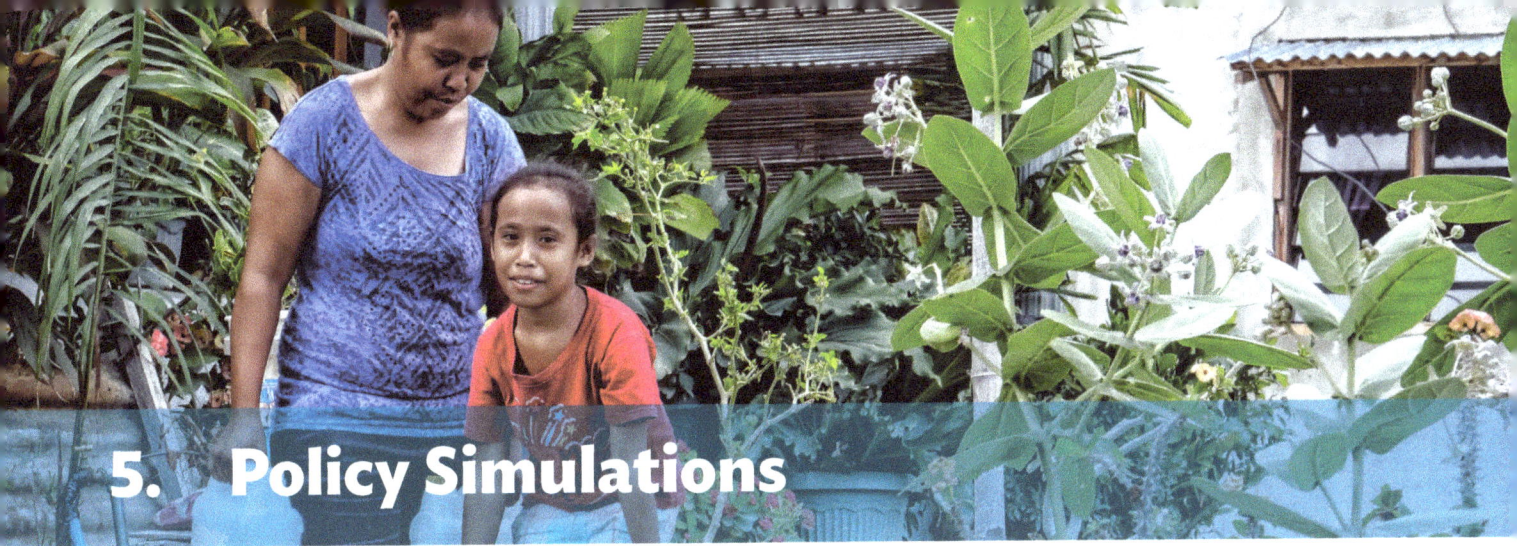

5. Policy Simulations

In addition to describing the incidence of existing taxes and expenditures, it is possible to use CEQ methods to simulate policy changes and assess their potential impact on poverty and inequality. This section examines several policy changes which are suggested by the results in the preceding section. None of the policies considered here is a concrete proposal of the government or anyone else. They are only presented in order to show how the CEQ assessment methods can be used to evaluate the distributional consequences of policy changes in different areas.

Bolsa da Mãe

The *Bolsa da Mãe* is a conditional cash transfer (CCT) program modeled after similar programs in many other developing countries. Its budget, at 0.3% of GNI, is a little lower than that found in other countries. However, its targeting is not as effective. Figure 6 shows the concentration coefficients for all countries with a CEQ assessment that also have a CCT scheme similar to Timor-Leste's.

Figure 6   Concentration Coefficients for Conditional Cash Transfer Programs, Selected from Countries with Completed Commitment to Equity Assessments

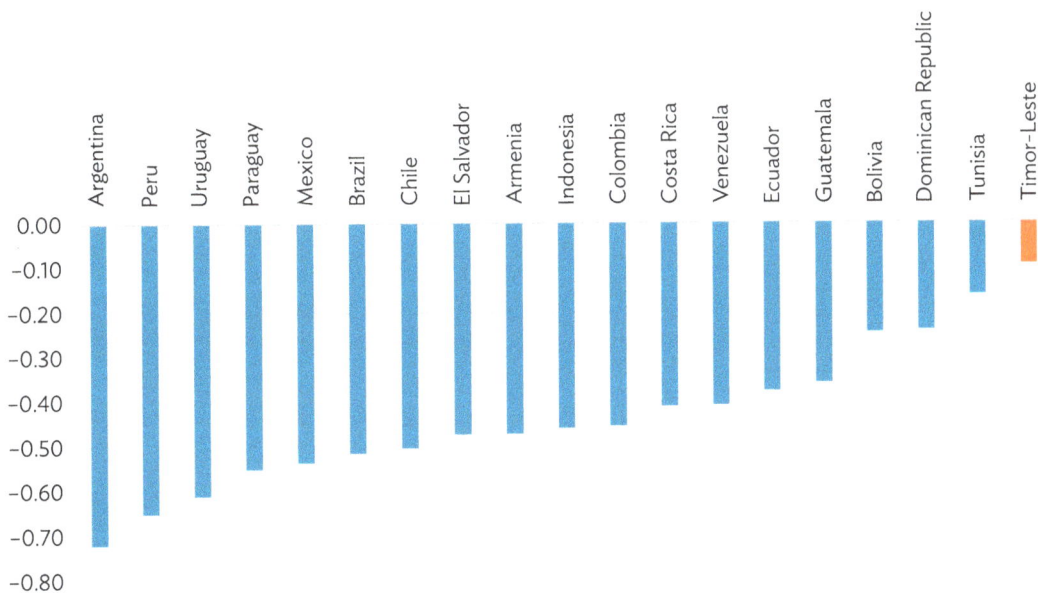

Source: Commitment to Equity. 2017. CEQ Standard Indicators. http://www.commitmentoequity.org/datacenter.

The *Bolsa da Mãe* has the lowest concentration among poor people of all of the cash transfer programs that have been considered in CEQ assessments. It is, therefore, interesting to ask to what extent Timor-Leste could reduce poverty and inequality by improving the targeting of *Bolsa da Mãe* toward poor people. Here, several targeting mechanisms are simulated. In addition, the amount of the transfer—$5 per child for up to three children—is small, especially taking into consideration the much larger size of pensions, like veterans' pensions. So increases in the size of the program are also simulated. The results of these simulations are presented in Table 8.[1]

Four simulations are presented. Simulation (1) assumes that the legislated targeting criteria are applied nationally and with exact knowledge of a household's income.[2] This is unrealistic, but it is a useful comparison to the actual distribution as it reflects "perfect" application of the current rules.

Simulation (2) attempts a more realistic approach to better targeting. Here, household consumption per capita is regressed on several variables that should be easy for a social worker to observe: the number of children in the household; whether the household head is female; whether the household is connected

Table 8   *Bolsa da Mãe* Simulations

Simulation	Current *Bolsa da Mãe*	(1)	(2)	(3)	(4)
Concentration coefficient	−0.055	−0.408	−0.299	−0.055	−0.091
Change in:					
• Inequality (Gini coefficient)		−0.005	−0.004	−0.003	−0.005
• Poverty (headcount)		0.010	0.000	−0.015	−0.009
• Poverty (gap)		−0.005	−0.004	−0.007	−0.009
• Size of the simulation ($ million)		0.0	0.0	10.1	10.1
Spending effectiveness	0.56	n.a.	n.a.	0.457	0.617

n.a. = not applicable.

Notes:

i.   Transfer values have been scaled up by the ratio of the administrative budget for *Bolsa da Mãe* in 2014 to the amount of *Bolsa da Mãe* benefits in the Timor-Leste Survey of Living Standards (TLSLS) data.

ii. Concentration coefficient calculated on disposable income less *Bolsa da Mãe* benefits, per capita.

iii. Size of the simulation refers to the net impact on the budget, in millions of dollars.

iv. Spending effectiveness is the reduction in the absolute poverty gap (in dollars) divided by the size of the simulation.

Description of simulations:

Simulation 1:   Distributes current amount of *Bolsa da Mãe* funds according to the legislated scoring formula, with household income per capita estimated exactly with TLSLS data.

Simulation 2:   Distributes current amount of *Bolsa da Mãe* funds according to a proxy means test that uses a regression of household expenditure per capita on the number of children in the household and whether the household: is headed by a woman; is connected to the electric grid; has good quality walls; is connected to a sewage line; is connected to the water mains; is urban; owns a car; and owns a refrigerator.

Simulation 3:   Doubles the amount of the current *Bolsa da Mãe* payment, from $5 per child to $10.

Simulation 4:   Same as simulation (2), but doubling the program size by expanding the recipient pool while keeping the payment at $5 per child.

Source: Timor-Leste Survey of Living Standards 2014/15 and authors' calculations.

---

[1]   One important feature of this and several of the ensuing simulations is that the transfers have been scaled up so that the total transfer in the survey is equal to the total amount in the administrative data (the budget). This is done because using the survey amounts only, which tend to be underreported, would yield smaller poverty effects and small program sizes (budgets) than should be expected, given the true size of the transfer.

[2]   In practice, a social worker estimates a household's income when assigning it an eligibility score. In addition, the scores are used within *sucos* (administrative units) to allocate a fixed amount of money made available to the suco, so it is possible for a household with a high eligibility score in one suco to not receive a transfer while a household with a lower score in another suco could receive it if its suco had relatively more funds or fewer qualifying households.

to the electricity grid, to piped water, and a flush toilet; whether the household has brick or concrete walls; whether the household owns a car; whether the household owns a refrigerator; the household's district; and whether the household is urban. Then the regression coefficients are used to create a household's predicted consumption per capita and use that prediction as a proxy means score (PMS). Households with lower scores (lower predicted consumption) qualify first for *Bolsa da Mãe*.

Simulation (3) doubles the amount that current *Bolsa da Mãe* recipients receive, from $5 per child per month to $10. Of course, this doubles the cost of the transfer.

Simulation (4) also doubles the size of the *Bolsa da Mãe* transfer, but rather than increasing current recipients' transfer, it expands the pool of recipients. Here the same PMS as in simulation (2) is used to determine who receives the transfer.

The first row of Table 8 shows the concentration coefficient for the simulated program. With the perfect application of the existing program criteria, simulation (1) would be much more concentrated among poor people than the current distribution of benefits, as expected. But it is not realistic to assume that social workers can identify a household's consumption exactly. Using an alternate PMS, simulation (2) also concentrates benefits more to poor people than the current program, though its concentration coefficient of -0.3 is still less negative than those for CCTs in other developing countries (Figure 6). Simulation (3) has exactly the same concentration coefficient as the current program since it just doubles current beneficiaries' transfer. Simulation (4) expands the program by adding more recipients based on the PMS of simulation (2). This concentration coefficient is less negative than simulation (2) because it includes more beneficiaries who are predicted to have a little more income than the beneficiaries in simulation (2), but it is still slightly better than the current distribution.

The next row of results shows the change in the Gini coefficient. This is always negative because each simulated program has a more negative concentration coefficient than the current program. Nevertheless, the improvements are small: between 0.003 and 0.006 points, or 1%–2%.[3]

The third row gives the change in the poverty headcount. The result for simulation (1) seems anomalous: this transfer is better-targeted to poor people than the current *Bolsa da Mãe*, but poverty actually increases by 1 percentage point. The explanation for this is that the current *Bolsa da Mãe* goes to many people who are just below the poverty line, not the poorest among poor people. As such, it moves many people above the poverty line, reducing the headcount. Perfect application of the program rules, as in simulation (2), would change the targeting to people further below the poverty line who do not manage to move above the poverty line after receiving the transfer. So the impact on the headcount is less.[4] Simulation (2) barely changes the poverty headcount for the same reason. Simulations (3) and (4) reduce the headcount by more—1.5 and 0.9 percentage points—but at the cost of doubling the program size from $10 million to $20 million. Note that doubling the payment to existing beneficiaries is slightly more effective at reducing the headcount than doubling the pool of beneficiaries.

The fourth row gives the change in the poverty gap. This is negative for all the simulations, but relatively small. Note that improvement in the poverty gap from better targeting, 0.004, is less than from increasing the program size, 0.007.

The next row gives the "size" of the simulation—how much the budget changes. The first two simulations just reallocate existing funds, so there is no net cost of implementing them. The last two double the program size from $10 to $20 million.

The last row gives one the measure of the effectiveness of additional spending: the reduction in the absolute poverty gap, which is a dollar amount, divided by the amount of extra spending. If all of a

---

3 Recall that the Gini coefficient for household consumption is 0.29.
4 This is why welfare economists do not like the headcount: it favors policies that benefit the least poor, rather than the poorest, among poor people.

program's additional spending went to poor people who stay poor, then all of it would reduce the poverty gap and this ratio would be one. Any spending that goes to nonpoor people, or that pushes a poor person beyond the poverty line rather than just to it, will reduce this ratio. Here, it may been seen that for simulation (3), a doubling of existing transfers, 46% of the additional spending would contribute to reducing the poverty gap, while for simulation (4), an expansion of the pool of recipients based on the alternate PMS, 62% of the spending would go to reducing the poverty gap. This is despite the fact that simulation (3) shows a larger reduction in the poverty *headcount*.

Improving targeting and building a more dynamic, comprehensive social registry is important for promoting pro-poor social spending, especially with shrinking fiscal resources. Simulations 1 and 2 show the improvements in targeting from the current distribution. However, the size of the transfer, at $5/child, is extremely low, which is why a big effect on poverty and inequality is not seen. In 2019, this was estimated to be 6% of average household budget of the poorest quintile or 2.7% of total consumption among all beneficiaries. Hence, improving targeting alone will not change poverty and inequality substantially. The government has approved an increase in the transfer amount. This, combined with improved targeting and more predictable and regular payments to current as well as new beneficiaries, will show benefits.

In the absence of improvements to targeting, an alternative social assistance strategy may be a universal basic income, a payment made to every person (or every child), regardless of need. Brown et al (2016) have advocated for such an approach in several African countries for the same reason. Nevertheless, the fiscal sustainability of a universal transfer remains a key concern for policymakers. Table 9 gives the results of several universal basic income simulations for Timor-Leste.

The first simulation uses only the current *Bolsa da Mãe* budget of $10 million but gives it to every citizen. Holding the budget constant requires a large reduction in the payment, to $0.69 per person per month. Compared to the current program, this would reduce inequality by a small amount and increase the poverty

rate by a small amount. Given the complete lack of targeting here, these are very small effects.

The second simulation gives the current *Bolsa da Mãe* transfer to every child (not every person) regardless of need. It is striking that the concentration coefficient and spending effectiveness for this simulation is identical to that for the existing (targeted) *Bolsa da Mãe* program. Just targeting children does as well as the current complicated criteria (Appendix I). Because this program keeps the payment constant and adds beneficiaries, it will cost government an extra $25.4 million per year, a significant increase of the *Bolsa da Mãe* budget, but still quite a lot smaller than the budget for veterans' pensions, and similar to the budget for retirement pensions (Table A1.4). But the extra money also generates much larger reductions in poverty (4.6 percentage points) and inequality (1.9 percentage points).

The third simulation expands the program even further by making a universal grant at the current $5 per month per person under the *Bolsa da Mãe*. This is much more expensive, costing an extra $63 million per year, about equal to the veterans' pension budget, but also generates much larger reductions in poverty and inequality. Still, its spending effectiveness is the lowest of any of the simulations reflecting the large share of a universal subsidy that would go to nonpoor people.

The fourth simulation tries to improve the targeting in a very simple way by limiting payments to children (as in simulation 2) but also excluding family members of anyone who is a formal sector worker. This has a slightly better concentration coefficient and spending effectiveness than the other simulations, and a much-reduced budget compared to either simulation (2) or (3).

The last simulation again targets children only, but doubles the payment for children under the age of 6 years old. This has targeting and spending effectiveness about the same as simulation (2)—targeting all children (and the current *Bolsa da Mãe* program)—but with a much larger budget to reflect both the larger number of beneficiaries and the larger payments to young children.

Of the universal basic income simulations results show that the one targeting all citizens (as opposed

Table 9   Universal Basic Income Simulations

Simulation	Current *Bolsa da Mãe*	(1)	(2)	(3)	(4)	(5)
Concentration coefficient /1	–0.055	0.000	–0.054	0.000	–0.157	–0.061
Change in:						
• Inequality (Gini coefficient)		–0.0111	–0.0193	–0.0087	–0.0149	–0.2595
• Poverty (headcount)		0.0032	–0.0457	–0.0932	–0.0242	–0.0672
• Poverty (gap)		0.0000	–0.0209	–0.0413	–0.0133	–0.0280
• Size of the simulation ($ million) /2		0.00	25.42	62.67	13.58	34.83
Spending effectiveness /3	0.56	n.a.	0.55	0.44	0.66	0.54

n.a. = not applicable.

Notes:

i.   Transfer values have been scaled up by the ratio of the administrative budget for Bolsa da Mãe in 2014 to the amount of Bolsa da Mãe benefits in the Timor-Leste Survey of Living Standards (TLSLS) data.

ii.   Concentration coefficient calculated on disposable income, per capita.

iii. Size of the simulation refers to the net impact on the budget in $ million.

iv.   Spending effectiveness is the reduction in the absolute poverty gap (in dollars) divided by the size of the simulation.

Description of simulations:

Simulation 1:   Distributes current amount of Bolsa da Mãe funds to everyone, with concomitant reduction in payment to $0.69 per person per month, with household income per capita estimated exactly with TLSLS data.

Simulation 2:   Distributes current amount of Bolsa da Mãe transfer to all children.

Simulation 3:   Distributes current amount of Bolsa da Mãe transfer to everyone.

Simulation 4:   Distributes current amount of Bolsa da Mãe transfer to all children in households where there is no formal sector worker.

Simulation 5:   Distributes current amount of Bolsa da Mãe transfer to all children, but doubled to $10 for children under 6 years old.

Source: Timor-Leste Survey of Living Standards 2014/15 and authors' calculations.

to children only) has less effective targeting or effectiveness than the current *Bolsa da Mãe* program. And only the one limiting benefits to children in families with a formal sector worker has better targeting and effectiveness. Any of the other options would perform about as well as the current program, but possibly at significantly reduced administrative costs since no screening of beneficiaries would be needed. Nevertheless, all of the simulations expand the beneficiary population which implies significant increases in program costs unless the already rather small benefit of $5 per person per month is reduced.

Electricity Subsidies

Electricity consumption is heavily subsidized in Timor-Leste. Households living outside Dili pay nothing for their electricity as their connections are not metered. Those living in Dili paid $0.05 per kilowatt-hour (kWh) for the first 20 kWh consumed and $0.12 thereafter in 2014, the year of the survey data.[5] Generation costs are expensive, in part because Timor-Leste must import all its fuel for generation and in part because the system is heavily overbuilt so depreciation costs are high. The average production cost is estimated at $0.27 per kWh, but that this cost could be as low as $0.21 per kWh if demand (mostly industrial) increased so as to make use of the system's excess capacity and if the fuel source were switched from diesel to fuel oil. For either estimate, the subsidy is large.

Table 10 gives the results of four simulated changes to electricity tariffs. The first charges current nonpayers (those who do not have meters, mostly in rural areas) the rates charged to Dili households:

---

[5]   That rate has since increased to $0.15 per kWh.

$0.05 for the first 20 kWh per month and $0.12 above that. The second charges current payers (those with meters in Dili) the full cost of their electricity, $0.21 per kWh, but continues to provide electricity for free in rural areas. The third charges everyone full cost. And the fourth charges everyone full cost, but then distributes the additional revenues to current *Bolsa da Mãe* recipients. Each of the first three simulations increases poverty with very little effect on inequality. The first two simulations increase poverty by 0.6 percentage points. Full cost recovery (simulation 3) would increase poverty by 1.7 percentage points, but raise about $12 million more in additional revenue.[6] The second simulation—raising tariffs for only those who currently have meters—is the most effective in the sense that only 17% of the revenue raised would come from poor people. This approach also reduces the concentration coefficient of the subsidy

somewhat, moving it more toward poorer households (because those who are unmetered, mostly in rural areas, are poorer than those who are metered).

The fourth simulation shows that even though electricity subsidies benefit poor people and removing them would increase poverty, they are not an effective way to reduce poverty. Here, subsidy is eliminated for everyone, as in the third simulation, but then distribute the additional revenue of $17 million to *Bolsa da Mãe* beneficiaries. This reduces the poverty headcount by 0.6 percentage points at no net cost to the budget.

One notable feature of Table 10 is that the amount of revenue raised in each simulation is small relative to the size of the loss government makes in the electricity sector (estimated at $53 million in 2016). In part, this is because capital costs of about $0.06 per kWh are

Table 10   Electricity Subsidy Simulations

Simulation	Current Electricity Subsidy	(1)	(2)	(3)	(4)
Concentration coefficient	0.261	0.291	0.187	n.a.	−0.054
Change in:					
• Inequality (Gini coefficient)		0.001	−0.001	0.001	−0.004
• Poverty (headcount)		0.006	0.006	0.017	−0.006
• Poverty (gap)		0.002	0.001	0.007	−0.003
• Size of the simulation ($ million)		−5.2	−5.8	−17.1	0.00
Spending effectiveness		−0.30	−0.17	−0.26	n.a.

n.a. = not applicable.

Notes:

i.   Concentration coefficient is calculated on disposable income less the veteran's pension, per capita.

ii.   Size of the simulation refers to the net impact on the budget, in millions of dollars.

iii. Spending effectiveness is the increase in the absolute poverty gap (in dollars) divided by the size of the simulation.

Description of simulations:

Simulation 1:   Current nonpayers are charged current rates to payers ($0.05/$0.12)

Simulation 2:   Current payers pay full cost of generation ($0.21); current nonpayers not charged.

Simulation 3:   All users pay full cost ($0.21).

Simulation 4:   All users pay full cost ($0.21); additional revenues distributed to *Bolsa da Mãe* beneficiaries.

Source: Timor-Leste Survey of Living Standards 2014/15 and authors' calculations.

---

[6]   Note that the amount of additional revenue calculated here is only what would come from households, which consume only about one-third of all electricity in Timor-Leste.

not included in calculation of the implicit subsidy, and in part, this is because a significant share of electricity is consumed by firms and the government rather than households.[7]

Increasing Wage Income Taxes

Income tax rates in Timor-Leste are low and include a very generous exemption amount: the first $500 of monthly income is not taxed, and any earnings above $500 are taxed at 10%. Here three changes to income taxes are simulated (Table 11). Simulation (1) lowers the exemption amount to $250 per month. Simulation (2) lowers it to three times the poverty line ($139 per month). And simulation (3) lowers it to twice the poverty line ($93) but also lowers the rate to 5% for incomes between two and three times the poverty line.

Given the progressivity of the wage income tax, it is surprising how much poverty the second and third simulations cause, with increases in the headcount of about a percentage point. In part, this is due to the large amount of revenue these policies raise. Increases in the poverty gap, however, are much smaller, indicating that the burden is not falling on the ex ante poor but rather those who were initially above the poverty line but fall below it with the policy change. The first simulation causes a much smaller increase in poverty, but also raises less revenue. The effectiveness of these changes is good, with only 16%–20% of the new tax burden falling on poor people.

There is a further simulation for wage income tax that cannot be addressed: raising the current rate for those earning over $500 per month (the current bracket limit). The TLSLS includes very few respondents who report incomes this high, far fewer than must exist because the income tax revenue that is inferred from the TLSLS data is much less than what the authorities

Table 11   Wage Income Tax Simulations

Simulation	Current Wage Income Tax	(1)	(2)	(3)
Concentration coefficient:	0.580	0.512	0.452	0.432
Change in:				
• Inequality (Gini coefficient)		−0.001	−0.001	−0.001
• Poverty (headcount)		0.003	0.009	0.011
• Poverty (gap)		0.001	0.002	0.003
• Size of the simulation ($million)		−3.3	−8.1	−9.9
Spending effectiveness		−0.16	−0.19	−0.20

Notes:
i.   Concentration coefficient calculated on disposable income per capita.
ii. Size of the simulation refers to the net impact on the budget, in millions of dollars.
iii. Spending effectiveness is the increase in the absolute poverty gap (in dollars) divided by the size of the simulation.

Description of simulations:
Simulation 1:   Bracket limit lowered from $500 to $250 per month.
Simulation 2:   Bracket limit lowered to triple the poverty line.
Simulation 3:   Bracket limit lowered to double the poverty line and rate lowered to 5%, with additional 10% bracket at triple the poverty line.

Source: Timor-Leste Survey of Living Standards 2014/15 and authors' calculations.

---

[7]   It is presumed that increased electricity costs to firms would be passed on to households, leading to somewhat larger poverty increases than those reported here. But lacking the information on the structure of production that would be found in supply and use tables or an input–output table, those indirect effects cannot be traced through to households consuming other goods and services.

actually collect. As a result, if an increase in the current tax rate were to be simulated for the same bracket, very little additional revenue would be yielded. Based on the discussion in Appendix I, it seems likely that such an increase would be highly progressive, more so than estimated with the TLSLS data.

Shifting to a Value-Added Tax

While most countries levy value-added tax (VAT) as their main source of indirect tax revenue, Timor-Leste's only broad-based indirect taxes are on imports: a 2.5% sales tax and a 2.5% import duty with limited exemptions which depend on the good imported and/or the importer. Table 12 presents results for several simulated changes to this approach. All the simulations assume that the sales tax and import duties would be eliminated, to be replaced by a VAT. They also all assume that with the exception of rice, food would be exempt, either by statute or because in

practical terms most food markets in Timor-Leste are informal and thus unlikely to be taxed. Rice is the only exception because it is imported in large quantities.

The first simulation imposes a VAT at a rate of 10% and assumes that the "collection effectiveness" —that is, the ratio of the amount the authorities collect over what actually should be paid—remains the same as the current regime. In effect, this doubles the amount of tax collected, yielding an additional $3.3 million in revenue. This has very little effect on inequality, but increases poverty by 0.3 percentage points.

The second simulation switches to a VAT at 5%, but assumes that the collection effectiveness is perfect— the authorities actually collect all that is due. This raises significantly more revenue, $9.8 million, but at the cost of a 1.1 percentage point increase in poverty.

The third simulation is identical to the second, but exempts rice. This improves the concentration coefficient by more than 11 percentage points, making the tax more progressive than the current regime. It

Table 12   Value-Added Tax Simulations

Simulation	Current Sales + Import Tax	(1)	(2)	(3)	(4)
Concentration coefficient /1	0.296	0.296	0.327	0.413	0.413
Change in:					
• Inequality (Gini coefficient)		0.000	−0.001	−0.001	−0.003
• Poverty (headcount)		0.003	0.011	0.007	0.014
• Poverty (gap)		0.001	0.003	0.001	0.004
• Size of the simulation ($ million) /2		3.3	9.8	6.4	16.2
Spending effectiveness /3		−0.23	−0.22	−0.14	−0.16

Notes:
i.   Concentration coefficient calculated on consumable income per capita.
ii.   Size of the simulation refers to the net impact on the budget, in millions of dollars.
iii.   Spending effectiveness is the increase in the absolute poverty gap (in dollars) divided by the size of the simulation.

Description of simulations:
Simulation 1:   Value-added tax (VAT) set at 10% on all purchases, sales and import duties eliminated, current collection effectiveness
Simulation 2:   VAT set at 5% on all purchases, food exempt except rice, sales and import duties eliminated, complete collection effectiveness
Simulation 3:   VAT set at 5% on all purchases, food exempt, sales and import duties eliminated, complete collection effectiveness
Simulation 4:   VAT set at 10% on all purchases, food exempt, sales and import duties eliminated, complete collection effectiveness

Source: Author's calculations

also raises $6.4 million more in revenue than current import taxes despite the rice exemption because of the assumption of perfect collection.

The final simulation is identical to the third, but with a 10% VAT rate. This raises $16.2 million in additional revenue (again, assuming perfect collection), but also increases poverty by 1.4 percentage points.

There are three interesting points about these simulations. First, if VAT could be collected effectively, it would yield considerable increases in revenue.[8] But it is not reasonable to expect perfect collection of any tax. So less revenue may be expected than is reported here (except in the first simulation), but

also less increase in poverty. Second, exempting rice from indirect taxation makes it considerably more progressive.

Perhaps the most unusual feature of these results is that once rice is exempted along with other food (simulations 3 and 4), indirect taxation becomes almost as progressive as direct taxation, and the spending effectiveness—how much of the additional tax collection comes from poor people—is actually slightly better than that for the direct tax simulations in Table 11. So the general rule of thumb that increasing direct taxation is more progressive than increasing indirect taxation does not hold in Timor-Leste, at least for the simulations presented here.

---

[8]   For that matter, the same is true of sales and import duties.

6. Conclusions

This assessment began with four questions about the distributional consequences of taxes and social expenditures in Timor-Leste:

(i) How much redistribution and income poverty reduction is being accomplished through revenue collection, social spending, and subsidies?

(ii) How progressive are revenue collection, subsidies, and government social spending?

(iii) How effective are revenue collection, subsidies, and government social spending at reducing inequality and poverty?

(iv) Within the limits of fiscal prudence, what could be done to increase redistribution and poverty reduction through changes in taxation and spending?

The answers to these questions reflect two unusual features of Timor-Leste's economy. First, Timor-Leste has natural resource revenues that are large relative to the rest of the economy. As a result, government spending is large relative to GDP for a low-income country, and the government is able to fund transfer payments that are more in line with an upper-middle income country. Since the majority of government expenditure is financed by the Petroleum Fund, what the government distributes to its citizens through social spending is much greater than what it takes from them in taxes. As a result, taxes and social spending reduce poverty by more in Timor-Leste than any other country with a CEQ assessment except Georgia.

The second unusual feature seen in Timor-Leste is that the income distribution is both dense and flat around the poverty line—there are a lot of people near the poverty line, both just below it and just above. This makes it difficult to target expenditures to poor people and taxes to nonpoor people. For example, the *Bolsa da Mãe*, Timor-Leste's conditional cash transfer (CCT) program, lags behind most similar programs in the countries for which CEQ has an assessment. Old age and disability pensions are less well-targeted, though that is a typical result in other countries as well.

The veterans' pension, targeted toward the combatants of the national independence struggle, is generous compared to other transfers. Since most recipients of veterans' pension often have little to no income, after receiving the pension, many veterans' households are moved well above the poverty line. Hence a reduction of poverty gap owed to the veterans' pension is more visible than any significant reduction in inequality.

The other large components of social expenditure, for education and health, are not meant to be strongly targeted to poor people but rather spread evenly over the population, which they are. Coverage, while not perfect, is very good for a low income country.

Overall, both direct taxes and transfer payments are less progressive in Timor-Leste than they are in other developing countries. This means that even though the budget reduces poverty by a lot, it has relatively little impact on inequality. Government taxation and social spending shift the income distribution quite a lot to the right, but do not compress it by much.

Measuring the "effectiveness" of a tax as the amount that it increases the poverty gap (roughly, the amount paid by poor people) over the total amount of the tax, direct taxes in Timor-Leste are found to be effective in the sense that poor people pay very little of them.

Indirect taxes are less effective, though the simulations do show that shifting to a value-added tax (VAT) that exempts food would make indirect taxation significantly more effective. This is due almost entirely to the exemption of rice, which currently pays sales tax and import duties, but would not pay VAT under a general food exemption. Indeed, these simulations are as effective as increasing the wage income tax by lowering the (quite high) bracket limit from $500 per month to two or three times the minimum wage.

Despite the excellent targeting of direct taxes, the marginal effects of taxes on inequality and poverty are small—less than 1 percentage point in every instance—because the tax take is also small (less than 1% of market income on average). Nevertheless, these taxes are "effective" in the sense that only a small share (10% or less) is collected from poor people.

On the expenditure side, effectiveness is measured in the same way, but is judged to be effective if a large share if it goes to poor people. None of the social expenditures examined are extremely effective by this measure. There is always a leakage of benefits to nonpoor people: 50% for veterans' pensions, 44% for *Bolsa da Mãe*, and more for old age and disability pensions.

What, if anything, can Timor-Leste do better? Improved targeting is important. Simulating different approaches to the *Bolsa da Mãe* shows that, it may be currently difficult to find administratively feasible methods to better target benefits to poor people, something that is also a result of the very flat and dense income distribution around the poverty line. However, social registries are a key instrument for policy management and the social and economic inclusion of the most vulnerable groups. Developing good social registries will help with the identification of those who need to be reached and the exploration of where possible gaps exist.

The electricity subsidy in Timor-Leste is large compared to social spending (Table A1.4). While removing the subsidy would increase poverty because poor people do benefit from it, subsidizing electricity may not always be an effective way to reduce poverty because much of the subsidy goes to nonpoor people. When savings from phasing out electricity subsidies to the general population are redirected to the poor through social assistance programs such as *Bolsa da Mãe*, poverty and inequality decreases without any additional cost to the budget.

It is not clear whether the government will need greater tax revenues in the medium term, but if it does, it has the option of increasing either direct or indirect taxes with relatively modest impact on poverty. While any tax increase must, by itself, increase poverty because it only takes funds from the population, the simulations find that only about 20% of additional tax revenue raised from either lowering the exempt amount for wage income tax or shifting from the current sales tax and import duties to a VAT would be drawn from poor people. In fact, if the VAT were to exempt food that is current taxed (mostly rice), the resulting tax would fall even less on poor people. At the same time, though, the amount of additional revenue that could be raised is relatively modest.

Overall, Timor-Leste has made great strides in its use of the budget to reduce poverty and increase the coverage of in-kind health and education benefits. The large budget share for transfers reduces poverty by more than in any other country with a CEQ assessment except Georgia. In-kind benefits of publicly provided health and education services whose coverage has expanded greatly also have strong effects on poverty reduction.

The results for inequality are more modest, in part because the income distribution is already equal, and in part because targeting expenditures to poor people and taxes to nonpoor people is difficult in Timor-Leste. The availability of funding from the Petroleum Fund means that this inability to target well is not too problematic for the moment since the government can compensate for it with relatively large social expenditures. However, over time, the government will need to find better ways to target its social expenditures if it wants to continue to have a strong effect on poverty while ensuring fiscal sustainability.

Appendix 1 Calculating the Commitment to Equity Income Variables and Their Components

Calculation of the Commitment to Equity (CEQ) income variables requires somewhat complex transformation of data from the Timor-Leste Survey of Living Standards 2014/15 (TLSLS) and administrative sources. Construction of the variables is described below and the spreadsheets and data files used are available upon request.

Construction of the Income and Expenditure Variables

Disposable Income

Construction of the CEQ income concepts starts with disposable income and works backward to market incomes and forward to final incomes (Figure 1). It is assumed that the welfare measure most commonly used from the TLSLS—household expenditure—is closest conceptually to disposable income. The expenditure variable as constructed by the General Directorate of Statistics (GDS) is used. There are theoretical arguments as to why a household's expenditure may best reflect its permanent income, but the motivation is mostly practical: in countries with a high degree of informal and self-employment, surveys like the TLSLS measure expenditures much more accurately than they measure incomes. To use this starting point, it is assumed that household net savings are zero, that is, disposable income is exactly equal to measured household expenditure.

Market Income

Market income plus pensions is constructed by summing disposable income and all direct taxes paid and subtracting all direct transfers received. Gross income and net market income follow directly, as shown in Figure 1.

The government makes several types of transfer payments in Timor-Leste and the TLSLS asks about them explicitly (section 12B) so it is possible to include most of them in the analysis. Pensions for older people (*pensão de idosos*) and people with disabilities (*pensão de invalidos*) are $30 per month. Every elderly person is entitled to a pension unless they receive another pension. To receive a disability pension, one must be between 18 and 60 years old and have a doctor certify the disability. The government also makes ad hoc transfers of cash, food, and building materials to families in temporary need, usually after disasters.

The *Bolsa da Mãe* is a conditional cash transfer program for mothers of children under 17 years old. The program is targeted based on a vulnerability scale that weighs a social worker's estimate of family income, the number of income earners in the household, the number of children, and the number of children with disabilities.[1] Funds are allocated to local administrative units (*sucos*) and then distributed within each suco according to the vulnerability score. The transfer is $5 per month per child, for up to three children per household.

For all of these transfers, the amounts that TLSLS respondents report receiving are sometimes inconsistent with the statutory amounts described here. In those cases, the amount is changed to the statutory amount, assuming that respondents' replies about the type of transfer received are accurate, but the reported amounts are not.

In addition to these cash transfers, government distributes actual goods under a variety of programs, which are termed quasi-cash transfers. The largest of these is the school meals program. Every child in public or private school gets a free meal in all basic,[2] primary, and junior secondary schools. The government also sometimes distributes free agricultural inputs (seeds, animals, vaccination services, equipment, and tools) to farmers; food (mostly rice and maize) to families deemed in need, usually after a disaster; mosquito nets and repair kits; and building materials or housing repair kits after disasters. For most of these transfers, the value of the goods reported by respondents is used, though for tractors a depreciation value assuming 10-year useful lives and an initial value of $2600 is used, and for boat motors a depreciation value assuming a 5-year useful life is used.[3]

Because market income is arrived at by subtracting transfers and pensions from disposable income (assumed equal to household consumption), it is possible that market income is negative if the household spent less money than the sum of its pensions and transfers (less any direct taxes it paid). In these cases, 1.6% of the total sample, it is assumed that the sum of pensions and transfers is, in fact, the correct estimate of disposable income, so all the income concepts are adjusted up by the difference between market and disposable income if market income is negative. This ensures that all the income concepts are non-negative. It does mean that the disposable income variable is slightly different from the GDS's household expenditure variable as it will be higher for households whose pensions and transfers are greater than their expenditures. As a consequence, the poverty estimates for disposable income will be slightly lower than the published poverty estimates.

Timor-Leste applies direct taxes to wages and salaries (wage income tax) and earnings from self-employment. Given the high degree of informality, it is assumed that only those wage or salary earners who are in the formal sector pay wage income tax. It is assumed that a job is formal if it is in the public sector; if the employee gets paid sick leave; if the employee has a written contract; or the employee reports paying tax on their earnings. A pretax wage is then worked out, based on respondents' reported earnings (which are assumed to be after tax) and the income tax schedule. The latter is very simple: there is an exemption up to $500 per month, and a flat 10% is charged on earnings over $500.

Also included as direct taxes are any amount that self-employed respondents report having paid in taxes (section 8e of the TLSLS questionnaire) and any amount the household reports having paid in taxes (section 4d of the TLSLS questionnaire).

---

[1]	The exact score is:	Household income:	6.25 points for income per capita between $300 and $456.25 per year
			12.50 points for income per capita between $200 and $300 per year
			18.75 points for income per capita between $100 and $200 per year
			25.00 points for income per capita less than $100 per year
		Household caregivers:	25 points for households with one or no caregivers
		Number of children:	12.50 points for single child households
			18.75 points for two child households
			25.00 points for three or more child households
		Handicapped children:	12.50 points for one handicapped child (mental or physical)
			25.00 points for two or more handicapped children

Households with higher scores get priority for the *Bolsa da Mãe*.

[2]   Basic schools (*eskolabasiku*) combine primary school, grades I–VI, with lower secondary, grades VII–IX.

[3]   Respondents report the value of a boat motor received, which is used. They do not report the value of a tractor received.

Consumable Income

To calculate consumable income, to the disposable income measure, indirect subsidies are added, and indirect taxes paid subtracted. The largest indirect subsidy by far in Timor-Leste is for electricity. It is the only one included in the analysis. Electricity is provided directly by the government. At the time of the TLSLS, the only households connected to the grid with meters were in Dili. All other households got electricity for free. Households in Dili, businesses, and government offices do pay, but at rates well below the cost of generation. For households, the rates were $0.05 for the first 20 kilowatt-hour (kWh) and $0.12 above that. Average cost of generation is extremely high, $0.27 per kWh, because the electricity system has over-capacity and relies on imported fuel. It is estimated that the cost of electricity generation could be as low as $0.21 per kWh if generation switched from diesel to cheaper heavy fuel oil. The subsidy is calculated as the difference between this latter cost estimate and what households actually pay so that excessive costs are not attributed as a subsidy to consumers.[4] Because the kWh consumed is estimated from households' reported expenditures on electricity (and the knowledge of the tariff structure), consumption by unmetered households who pay nothing cannot be directly inferred. For them, use is estimated as the average kWh consumed by metered households—those that do report expenditures on electricity—in the same percentile of the income distribution.

Indirect taxes in Timor-Leste include import duties of 2.5%; sales tax of 2.5% levied only on imports; a services tax of 5% levied on telephone services, restaurants, and hotels; and a variety of excises, including on petroleum products, alcoholic beverages, and tobacco products.[5] Households do not pay these taxes explicitly, but they are reflected in the prices they pay for taxed goods and services. To estimate how much a household has paid implicitly when purchasing goods and services, the statutory rates are applied to the reported expenditures (or physical quantities purchase in the case of excises), taking into account the limited exemptions available. For the services tax, only expenditures on telephone services are included because most spends on hospitality services are incurred at restaurants and hotels run by informal providers who most likely do not pay the tax.

Table A1.1   Timor-Leste Excise Duty Rates, 2014

Item	Rate
Petrol and diesel	$0.06 per liter
Beer	$1.90 per liter
Wine	$2.50 per liter
Spirits	$8.90 per liter
Cigarettes	$19.00 per kilogram

Source: Democratic Republic of Timor-Leste. 2008. Law No. 8/2008. Lei Tributaria. Dili.

Final Income

To calculate final income, in-kind transfers associated with public provision of education and health care are added to consumable income. This step is important because these items are a large share of social spending in Timor-Leste, but it is difficult because these services are provided free-of-charge to recipients.[6] To estimate the value of these services to recipients, the government's total recurrent cost of provision for schooling is calculated by level (pre-primary, basic, senior secondary, tertiary, and vocational) and health care by type of service (inpatient or outpatient). The total cost is then divided by the number of beneficiaries, and it is assumed that each beneficiary receives the average amount of benefit. This is the standard approach in benefit-incidence studies (Demery, 2003), but it is better understood as "expenditure" incidence, since it neither accounts for differences in the quality of services across different providers nor takes into account differences in the value that recipients themselves place on these services. Table A1.2 gives the estimated value per beneficiary.

---

[4] This is a slight underestimate of the true subsidy because the indirect effect of subsidized electricity on the prices of goods and services that use electricity as an input cannot be accounted for. Some CEQ analyses do make this calculation, but it requires an input–output table which does not exist for Timor-Leste. In any event, the production structure in Timor-Leste is sufficiently simple that these indirect effects are likely to be small.

[5] Table A1.1 gives the excise rates

[6] Except for university education, which requires a fee of $30 per term.

Table A1.2   Cost-of-Provision for Free and Subsidized Health and Education Services

Service		Cost per Beneficiary, National Average
Pre-primary school	Public	$93 per year
	Private	$32 per year
Basic school	Public	$140 per year
	Private	$40 per year
Senior secondary school	Public	$144 per year
	Private	$102 per year
University	Public	$700 per year
	Private	$83 per year
Outpatient health care in hospitals		$17.77 per visit
Outpatient health care in district clinics and health posts		$7.99 per visit
Outpatient care in mobile clinics		$3.60 per visit
Inpatient health care in hospitals		$112.84 per day

Source: Ministries of Education, Health, and Finance, Government of Timor-Leste and authors' calculations

The government of Timor-Leste supports both public and private schools.[7] The largest expense by far is for teachers' salaries. The government pays teachers in public schools, of course, but there are also teachers in private schools (barring universities) who are public functionaries seconded to those schools. While the Ministry of Education does not know exactly how many such teachers there are, it estimates that about 30% of teachers in private schools are actually public functionaries. To calculate the per student expenditure at each type of school, the total number of public school students (by school level) was first added to 30% of the number of private school students to get a total student population who are served by public teachers. Then 77% (1/1.3) of the total wage bill was allocated to public school students and 23% (0.3/1.3) to private school students. The expenditures for goods and services (which apply only to public schools) and concessional grants (which are reported by school type) were then added to this amount to get total spending for public and private schools, by level. Finally, those total budgets were divided by the number of students recorded by the Ministry of Education to get the per student benefit by school type.

The TLSLS questionnaire allows us to identify four different types of publicly provided health care: inpatient care at hospitals (including the number of days as an inpatient); outpatient care at hospitals; outpatient care at district health facilities (community health centers and health posts); and outpatient care at mobile clinics. The budget information, however, is available only by type of institution (hospital, district health facility, or mobile clinic) as well as aggregate budgets across all facilities for all diagnostic services and medicines. To allocate the institutional budgets, it is assumed that district health facilities and mobile clinics only provide outpatient services, so all of their budgets are allocated to outpatient services.[8] For hospitals, it is estimated that 72% of hospital expenditures went to inpatients and 16 went to outpatients.[9] These shares were updated using data on the share of expenditures (including diagnostic services and medicines) in 2014, to 80.25% and 18.40%, respectively, and applied to the total hospital budget for 2014 to get spending on inpatients and outpatients at hospitals. It is assumed that all diagnostic services are obtained in hospitals, and divide that budget in the same shares among

[7]   "Private," "religious," and "community" schools are combined as private schools in the analysis.

[8]   In fact, there are very few inpatients at district health facilities and none at mobile clinics.

[9]   Government of Timor-Leste. 2007. Hospital Costing Study: Hospital National Guido Valadares, Bacau, Maliana, Maubisse, and Oecusse and Suai Referral Hospitals. Unpublished Report by the Ministry of Health. Dili.

hospital inpatients and outpatients. Finally, the budget for medicines is distributed equally among all patients regardless of facility. Adding up these three items—the budget for facilities, diagnostic services, and medicines— gives total expenditure for the four types of services identified above. Those totals are divided by the Ministry's recorded number of visits to each type of facility for outpatient services and by the number of inpatient days for inpatient services. That yields the unit costs reported in Table A1.2.

Because almost all health and education services are free of charge in Timor-Leste,[10] reported fees paid are not subtracted from the estimated benefit except for university tuition which is $30 per semester.

Consistency between Administrative and Survey Data Sources

It is possible to calculate government spends on certain items and taxes on others using both TLSLS data as well as administrative data (national accounts, budget, etc.). Because the TLSLS is a nationally representative survey, these amounts should coincide, but they often do not. This can lead to errors in the estimated distributional effects if the degree of inconsistency varies among the tax, expenditure, and income variables used in the analysis. For example, suppose that the total value of *Bolsa da Mãe* benefits in the survey is only half of the amount found in the budget, perhaps because survey respondents are reluctant to report that they receive these benefits. If those benefits go disproportionately to poorer households, which seems likely, then their underreporting in the survey would cause us to underestimate the impact that these benefits have on both inequality and poverty reduction. It is important to keep these possibilities in mind when considering the results.

Table A1.3 gives these comparisons for revenues. As noted in the text, it is possible to analyze only those items for which the tax payer can be identified in the TLSLS data, limiting us to wage income tax and most indirect taxes. For every tax possible to include in the analysis, the estimate of the total tax paid from the TLSLS in column 4 is much less than the amount recorded in the budget. It is important to consider the causes of these differences in order to understand how they affect the analysis in the text.

For wage income tax, the revenue authorities report $16 million in 2014, while the calculations from the TLSLS yield only $2 million. Evidently, there are high income individuals who have not responded to the TLSLS. It is fairly common for this to happen in surveys as rich households refuse to respond, but the refusal rates in the TLSLS were very low, less than 1%, so that is unlikely to be the problem. It is possible that these few high income individuals happened not to be sampled, something that appears to be part of the explanation.

It is possible to do a little more with this, however. The revenue authorities report that $9 million of the $16 million in wage income tax comes from the public sector. In the TLSLS, however, public sector employees report wages that would only yield about $0.5 million in wage income tax. This could be because public sector employees underreport their wages in the TLSLS, but that does not seem to be the case. Ministry of Finance data on the number of public sector employees at each pay grade was compared with the number of TLSLS respondents who work in the public sector and the pay grade they fall into. Figure A1.1 shows that the TLSLS actually reports more civil servants in the *highest* pay grade than found in the payroll data.

Instead, it seems that a large share of public sector wages goes to workers who are not on the payroll and may not have responded to the TLSLS. The total payroll in 2014 was $150 million, plus an

---

10   University education and VIP (high-end) hospital rooms are exceptions.

Table A1.3   Government Revenues, Actual Budgets, and TLSLS Estimates

	Amount ($ million)	Share (%) of GNI	Amount estimated in TLSLS ($ million)	Amount as a percentage of Market Income (as per TLSLS)	Ratio of TLSLS Estimate to Actual Budget Amount
Total Revenue & Grants	1,162	34.7			
• Revenue	900	26.9			
○ Tax revenue	124	3.7			
– Direct taxes, *of which*	53	1.6			
■ Personal income tax	0	0.0	0	0.0	
■ Payroll tax (Wage income tax)	16	0.5	2	0.3	0.15
■ Corporate income tax	8	0.2			
■ Withholding tax	28	0.8			
■ Taxes on property	0	0.0			
– Contributions to social insurance	0				
– Indirect taxes, *of which*	71	2.1			
■ Sales tax	15	0.4	2	0.2	0.12
■ Customs duties	13	0.4	2	0.2	0.12
■ Services tax	3	0.1	1	0.1	0.17
■ Excise duties, *of which:*	40	1.2			
□ Petrol	10	0.3	1	0.1	0.07
□ Beer	12	0.4			
□ Wine	1	0.0			
□ Spirits	1	0.0			
□ Tobacco	14	0.4			
○ Nontax revenue	776	23.2			
– Transfers from Petroleum Fund	732	21.9			
– Other nontax revenue	44	1.3			
• Grants	262	7.8			
Share of tax revenues included in analysis		53.3			
Share of revenues, transfers, and grants included		5.7			
Revenues included in analysis as a percentage of GNI		2.0		1.0	

GNI = Gross National Income, TLSLS = Timor-Leste Survey of Living Standards 2014/15.

Source: Ministry of Finance, Government of Timor-Leste.

additional $73 million in personal service contracts for consultants. The TLSLS total for public sector workers is $146 million, so the difference is about $77 million, almost all of which would have been paid to consultants, many of whom are foreign and so do not respond to the TLSLS. Assuming their salaries are high, their wages would yield about $7 million in wage income tax, largely accounting for the difference between the revenue authorities' figure for wage income tax and that in the TLSLS. That still leaves about $5 million unaccounted for, which many only be attributed to either bad luck on sampling richer households or underreporting of wage income by some private sector households.

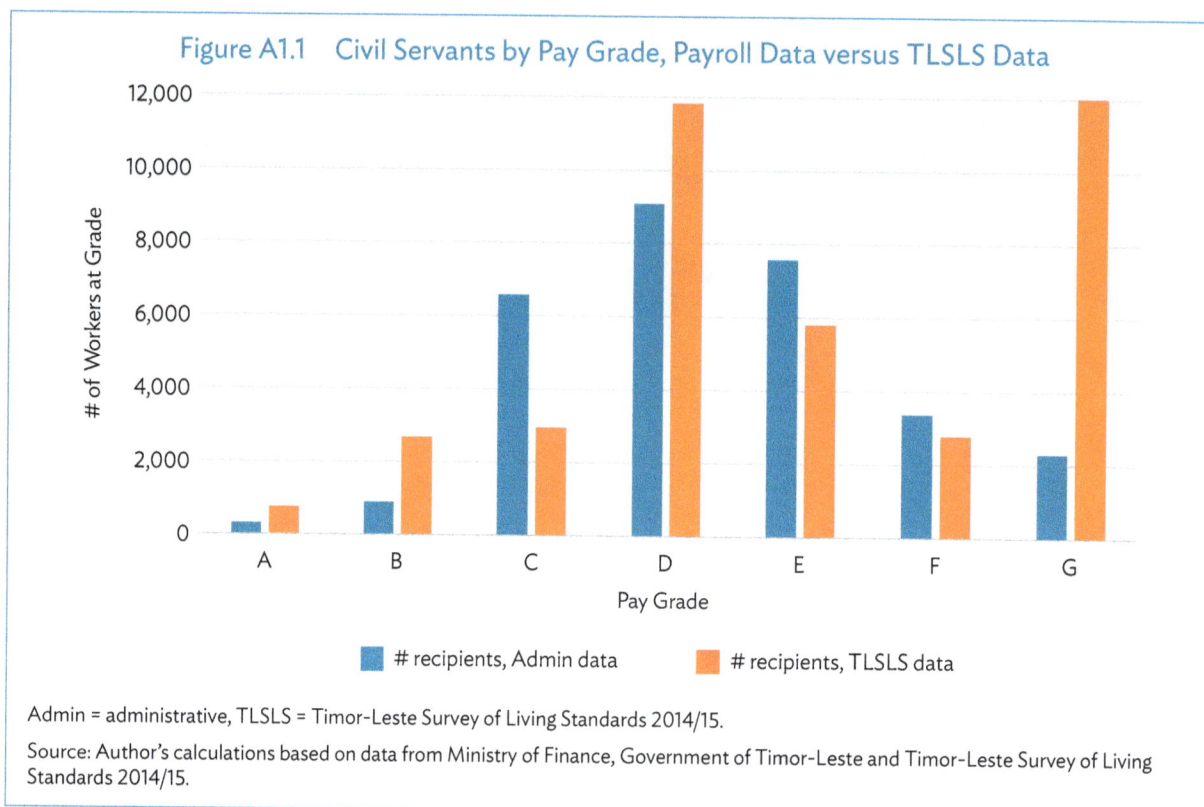

Figure A1.1   Civil Servants by Pay Grade, Payroll Data versus TLSLS Data

Admin = administrative, TLSLS = Timor-Leste Survey of Living Standards 2014/15.

Source: Author's calculations based on data from Ministry of Finance, Government of Timor-Leste and Timor-Leste Survey of Living Standards 2014/15.

What are the implications of this information for the results presented in the text? The most important one is that the wage income tax is surely more progressive than reported in Table 4. So direct taxation probably has a greater effect at reducing inequality than reported. On the other hand, the poverty consequences of wage income tax in Table 4 should be accurate: the people who are paying the "missing" wage income tax are, by definition, high income. Taxing them will not increase poverty. In addition, as noted in the simulations section, while the consequences of an increase in the tax rate on currently paying individuals (with monthly wage income over $500) cannot be assessed properly, that would certainly be more progressive than any of the simulations reported, all of which focus on lowering the bracket limit and thus bringing more middle class people into the tax net.

Table A1.3 also shows that sales tax and import duties calculated in the TLSLS are much lower than those reported in the budget. But those taxes are levied on all imports, including those purchased by government and by firms. While the shares of imports purchased by households are not known, the share of gross national expenditure is (34%). But much of those purchases are food which, with the exception of rice, is mostly produced domestically and thus not taxed. Taking this into account, households actually consume only 13% of the likely tax base for sales tax and import duties. That is almost exactly the ratio of the TLSLS-calculated sales tax and import duties to the administrative accounts in the last column. So the TLSLS expenditure data actually seem to be quite accurate.

Nevertheless, the calculation of the incidence of sales tax and import duties probably is not accurate because firms will pass on the amounts they pay in these taxes on their intermediate goods in the prices they charge. It is possible to capture these indirect effects of the sales tax and import duties, but only if there is an input–output table or tables from the national accounts are used.[11] But these are not available in Timor-Leste.

---

[11]   See Jellema and Inchauste, 2017.

The fact that these indirect effects are a large share of the total tax take for sales tax and import duties means that the analysis in the text underestimates both the revenue raised (as seen in Table A1.3) and the poverty implications because the indirect effects will spill over to goods and services consumed by poor people. On the other hand, the estimated effect on inequality is likely to be accurate since the indirect effects are (probably) similarly distributed to disposable income (household consumption in general).

Finally, all of the estimated revenue for excises from the TLSLS is lower than found in the budget data. For petrol, this is because most petrol is not consumed by households, but by firms. As with sales tax and import duties, it would be good to be able to trace the indirect effects through the production structure, but that is not possible in Timor-Leste. This means that the poverty impact of petrol duties is likely underestimated.

For alcohol and tobacco, survey respondents typically underreport their consumption of these goods, often substantially. It is impossible to know who is underreporting and by how much, so not much can be said about how this biases the results other than to say that, again, the poverty consequences of these taxes are likely to be larger than estimated.

Table A1.4 gives information on the expenditure side of the budget. Survey information is usually more accurate for expenditures, and this is true for the most part in Timor-Leste. Nevertheless, there are some differences that require discussion.

Three of the transfer payments—*Bolsa da Mãe*, veterans' pensions, and other cash payments (which are mostly for disaster relief)—are significantly lower in the TLSLS than they are in the budget. It is not clear why this is the case, but it may reflect respondents' fear that they could lose their benefit. Since each of these transfers tends to go more to poor people, it

is likely that their impact on poverty and inequality is underestimated in the text even though those estimated effects are already large.

The difference for "rice and other food" probably reflects the fact that most of this budget is used to subsidize rice, but the study has not modeled that. The only part of this budget captured is food that is distributed for free, as reported by respondents. This, too, is usually in response to disasters.

There is also a large discrepancy between the budgeted amount for university education and the amount calculated in the TLSLS. This is due to a large difference in the number of public university students. The Ministry of Education reports 17,744 students at the National University but the TLSLS records only 5,011. This difference cannot be explained as there is no obvious reason why respondents would be reluctant to report attending the university. As with the high wage incomes, it may just be that university students, who are relatively few in the population, just happened not to be sampled.

Finally, there is a large discrepancy between the budgeted electricity subsidy and the amount calculated from the TLSLS. There are two sources for this. First, the budgeted subsidy includes capital expenditures. These were excluded from the subsidy calculation because the electricity grid is already overbuilt so these expenditures would not seem to be a benefit to current consumers. Second, firms and the government also consume electricity, though the shares are not known. As with the indirect taxes, to the extent that firms use subsidized electricity, they may pass the subsidy along in lower prices for their goods and services, thus benefiting households indirectly. This means that the poverty reduction effects of the electricity subsidy are likely underestimated, though the inequality effects should be accurate as the distribution of the indirect benefits probably is similar to household consumption in general.

Table A1.4 Government Expenditures, Actual Budgets, and TLSLS Estimates

	Amount ($million)	Share (%) of GNI	Amount estimated in TLSLS ($million)	Amount as a percentage of Market Income (as per TLSLS)	Ratio of TLSLS Estimate to Actual Budget Amount
Total Expenditure	1,339	40.0			
• Defense spending	24	0.7			
• Social spending	377	11.3			
º Social protection	137	4.1			
– Social assistance *of which*	112	3.4			
▪ Cash transfers, *of which*	17	0.5			
▫ Bolsa da Mãe	10	0.3	4	0.6	0.43
▫ Other cash payments	7	0.2	4	0.5	0.58
▪ Noncontributory Pensions	96	2.9			
▫ Old age pension	32		30	3.8	0.92
▫ Disability pension	3	0.1	4	0.5	1.60
▫ Veteran's pension	61	1.8	41	5.2	0.67
▪ Near cash transfers	22	0.7			
▫ School meals	14	0.4	14	1.8	1.04
▫ Rice and other food	8	0.3	0	0.0	0.01
▪ Other	4	0.1			
º Education, *of which*	176	5.3			
– Pre-school	1	0.0	1	0.1	0.74
– *Eskolabasiku*	40	1.2	45	5.7	1.13
– Secondary	6	0.2	7	0.8	1.20
– Vocational	18	0.5			
– Tertiary	15	0.5	4	0.5	0.22
º Health, *of which*	64	1.9			
– Outpatient, *of which*	28	0.8	17	2.1	0.60
▪ at hospitals		0.0	5	0.6	
▪ at district health facilities		0.0	11	1.5	
▪ at mobile clinics		0.0	0	0.0	
– Inpatient	15	0.4	10	1.3	0.68
– Other health	22	0.7			
º Housing & urban, *of which*	11	0.3			
– home repairs and materials	1	0.0	1	0.1	1.26
• Subsidies, *of which*	101	3.0			
º Electricity	101	3.0	11	1.5	0.11
Share of expenditures included in analysis		25.4			
Expenditures included in analysis as a percentage of GNI		9.2		26.1	

GNI = Gross National Income, TLSLS = Timor-Leste Survey of Living Standards 2014/15.

Source: Ministries of Finance, Agriculture, Education, and Health, Government of Timor-Leste.

Appendix 2 Measures of Inequality, Poverty, and Incidence

There are many measures of inequality, poverty, and incidence of which this assessment uses only a few. For inequality, the Gini coefficient is used. For poverty, the Foster–Greer–Thorbecke (FGT) poverty measures are used. For incidence, concentration coefficients and the marginal effect of a tax or expenditure on poverty and inequality are used. Finally, for effectiveness, the Commitment to Equity (CEQ) spending effectiveness measure for the poverty gap is used.

Inequality Measurement by Gini Coefficient

The Gini coefficient is by far the most common inequality measure. The easiest way to understand it is to first construct a Lorenz curve: order the data by income, from poorest to richest and then graph the cumulative share of the sample on the horizontal axis against the cumulative share of income on the vertical axis. Table A2.1 gives some example data for 10 people. Since there are 10 people, the first person represents 10% of the sample, the first two people represent 20%, etc., as given in column 2. Column 3 gives each person's income and it may be seen that the data are ordered from poorest to richest. The sum of all the incomes is 1,000, so the income shares (column 4) are arrived at by dividing each person's income by 1,000. Finally, column 5 gives the cumulative income shares. The Lorenz curve graphs column 5 against column 2, as in Figure A2.1. Note that because both axes are shares, they range from zero to one.

Table A2.1 Example Data for a Lorenz Curve and Gini Coefficient

Observation	Cumulative Population Share	Income	Income Share	Cumulative Income Share
1	0.100	1	0.001	0.001
2	0.200	3	0.003	0.004
3	0.300	7	0.007	0.011
4	0.400	13	0.013	0.024
5	0.500	20	0.020	0.044
6	0.600	30	0.030	0.074
7	0.700	60	0.060	0.134
8	0.800	100	0.100	0.234
9	0.900	250	0.250	0.484
10	1.000	516	0.516	1.000
	Total:	1,000		

Because the data are ordered from poorest to richest, the Lorenz curve must be convex: the poorest person's share cannot be greater than his or her population share, and so on for the poorest two people, etc. In fact, the more convex the Lorenz curve, the more unequal the distribution of income. In the extreme case in which one person has all the income, the Lorenz curve would be a right angle, running along the horizontal axis until it reaches the last person in the sample because everyone but that person would have zero income. On the other hand, if everyone has exactly the same income—complete equality—the cumulative income share is equal to the cumulative population share and the Lorenz curve is a 45-degree line.

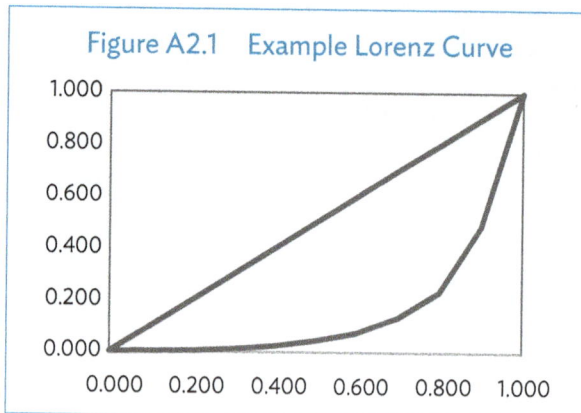

Figure A2.1   Example Lorenz Curve

Poverty Measurement Using Foster–Greer–Thorbecke Measures

The most common poverty measures are the FGT measures. This is a group of related measures. The first is the "headcount" which is just the share of the population that is poor. The second is the "poverty gap" which is the average difference between the poverty line and a person's income, usually scaled by the poverty line itself:

$$poverty\ gap = \left(\frac{1}{N}\right) \cdot \sum_{i} \left(\frac{z - y_i}{z}\right)_+$$

where z is the poverty line, y_i is the ith person's income, and N is the sample size. The plus sign indicates that the difference is only included if it is positive. The third FGT measure is the squared poverty gap, sometimes called "poverty severity." It is like the poverty gap but with the term in parentheses squared.[1]

The Gini coefficient is the area between the 45-degree line and the Lorenz curve, multiplied by two. In the case of complete equality, the Lorenz curve would be on the 45-degree line so the Gini coefficient is zero. For complete inequality, the Gini is twice the triangle below the 45-degree line, or one. In practice, Gini coefficients in the most equal countries are around 0.25 while those for the most unequal countries are around 0.70.

Table A2.2   Foster–Greer–Thorbecke Measure of Poverty: An Illustration

Observation	Income	Poor?	Absolute Poverty Gap	Scaled Poverty Gap	Scaled Poverty Gap Squared
1	1	1	20	0.952	0.907
2	3	1	18	0.857	0.735
3	7	1	14	0.667	0.444
4	13	1	8	0.381	0.145
5	20	1	1	0.048	0.002
6	30	0	0	0	0
7	60	0	0	0	0
8	100	0	0	0	0
9	250	0	0	0	0
10	516	0	0	0	0
Sum:		5		2.90	2.23
Average (FGT)		0.50		0.29	0.22
Poverty line		21			

---

[1]   In fact, the "family" of FGT measures can be written concisely as:

$$FGT(\alpha) = \left(\frac{1}{N}\right) \cdot \sum_{i} \left(\frac{z - y_i}{z}\right)_+^{\alpha}$$

If $\alpha = 0$, the term in parentheses is 1 if a person is poor, 0 otherwise, so that gives us the headcount. If $\alpha = 1$, the poverty gap is arrived at, and if $\alpha = 2$, poverty severity is measured.

Table A2.2 gives an example of the FGT calculation for the same data used to derive the Lorenz curve and assuming that the poverty line is 21. Column 3 just indicates whether or not a person is poor. Summing it and dividing by the sample size gives the headcount: 0.50—so half the population is poor. Column 4 gives the absolute poverty gap for each person: the difference between the poverty line (21) and her/his own income. This has an interesting interpretation as it shows how much money would be needed to bring every person (just) out of poverty. Column 5 scales each person's absolute poverty gap by the poverty line. Averaging that over the sample gives the poverty gap: 0.29. Finally, column 6 squares each person's scaled poverty gap. Averaging that gives poverty severity: 0.22.

Incidence: Concentration Curves and Coefficients

A concentration curve is similar to a Lorenz curve. The data is ordered from poorest to richest and then the cumulative share plotted, of a tax or benefit against the cumulative share of the population. Table A2.3 provides example data for a tax paid and Figure A2.2 shows the corresponding curve which graphs column 6 against column 2.

Unlike a Lorenz curve, a concentration curve can be either convex or concave. The latter would occur if poorer people paid a higher share of a tax than rich people (which is highly unlikely) or receive a higher share of a benefit than rich people (which may well be the case for explicitly targeted transfers).

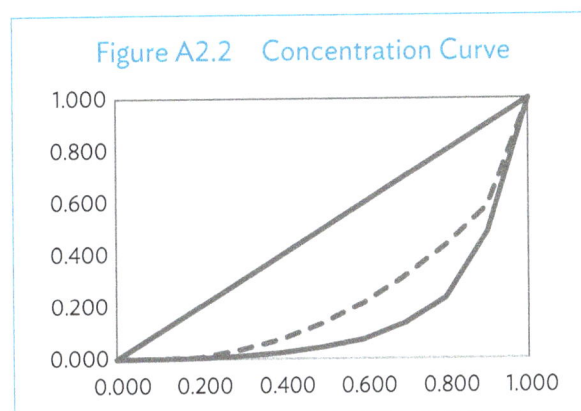

Figure A2.2   Concentration Curve

Table A2.3   Example Data for a Concentration Curve

Observation	Cumulative Population Share	Income	Tax Paid	Tax Share	Cumulative Tax Share
	0.000				0.000
1	0.100	1	0.1	0.001	0.001
2	0.200	3	0.4	0.004	0.005
3	0.300	7	3.0	0.030	0.035
4	0.400	13	4.0	0.040	0.075
5	0.500	20	6.0	0.060	0.135
6	0.600	30	8.0	0.080	0.215
7	0.700	60	10.0	0.100	0.315
8	0.800	100	12.0	0.120	0.435
9	0.900	250	15.0	0.150	0.585
10	1.000	516	41.5	0.415	1.000
Total		1,000	100		

Like the Gini coefficient, the concentration coefficient for a tax or expenditure is the area between its concentration curve and the 45-degree line. This can range from negative one (the poorest person only pays all the tax or receives all the benefit) to one (the richest person pays all the tax or receives all the benefit), with zero representing a tax or benefit spread evenly across the population. Taxes are usually referred to as regressive if their concentration coefficient is less than the Gini coefficient, i.e., their concentration curve is less convex (closer to the 45-degree line), and progressive if the concentration coefficient is greater than the Gini. So the example in Figure A2.2 is for a regressive tax. Those expenditures that have a concave concentration curve (negative concentration coefficient) are referred to are referred to as "pro-poor" or "absolutely pro-poor." Those with a concentration curve below the Lorenz curve (concentration coefficient greater than the Gini) are "regressive." And expenditures with a concentration curve between the Lorenz curve and the 45-degree line (concentration coefficient less than the Gini, but positive) as "relatively pro-poor."

Incidence: Marginal Effects on Poverty and Inequality

Another way to assess the incidence of a particular tax or expenditure item is to see how it alone changes poverty or inequality. The CEQ framework calls this the "marginal effect" of the tax or expenditure. To calculate it, a measure of inequality or poverty is calculated for a CEQ income concept (any of those given in Figure 1) and then the same inequality or poverty measure is recalculated after either adding or removing the tax or expenditure item of interest. The difference in the two measures is the "marginal effect."

One important difference between the marginal effect and the concentration coefficient is that the marginal effect depends on the overall size of the tax or expenditure while the concentration coefficient does not. A larger transfer, for example, can have a larger impact on inequality and especially poverty than a smaller one that is distributed to exactly the same people and so has the same concentration curve.

Effectiveness: Measuring "Bang for the Buck"

The last measure considered is the "effectiveness" of a tax or spending item. There are several such measures (Enami, 2018), but in this report the spending effectiveness of the poverty gap is used. For expenditures, this is the total decrease in the absolute poverty gap divided by the total amount of the expenditure item. If all of the expenditure goes to poor people and does not move them above the poverty line, then it will all serve to reduce the poverty gap, and this measure equals one. On the other hand, if all of the expenditure goes to nonpoor people, the poverty gap will not change and the spending effectiveness measure equals zero. For taxes, the measure is similar, but its interpretation is reversed. If all of a tax falls on poor people, then the absolute poverty gap will increase by the amount of the tax and the spending effectiveness measure will be one, while if none of the tax falls on poor people, the measure will be zero.

Coverage

The last concept used in this report is "coverage." This measures the total number of beneficiaries of an expenditure or program (or payers of a tax) divided by the target population for that benefit or tax. This denominator may be the entire population, or some subset. For example, for retirement pensions, the ratio of people receiving such pensions is divided by the population older than 60.

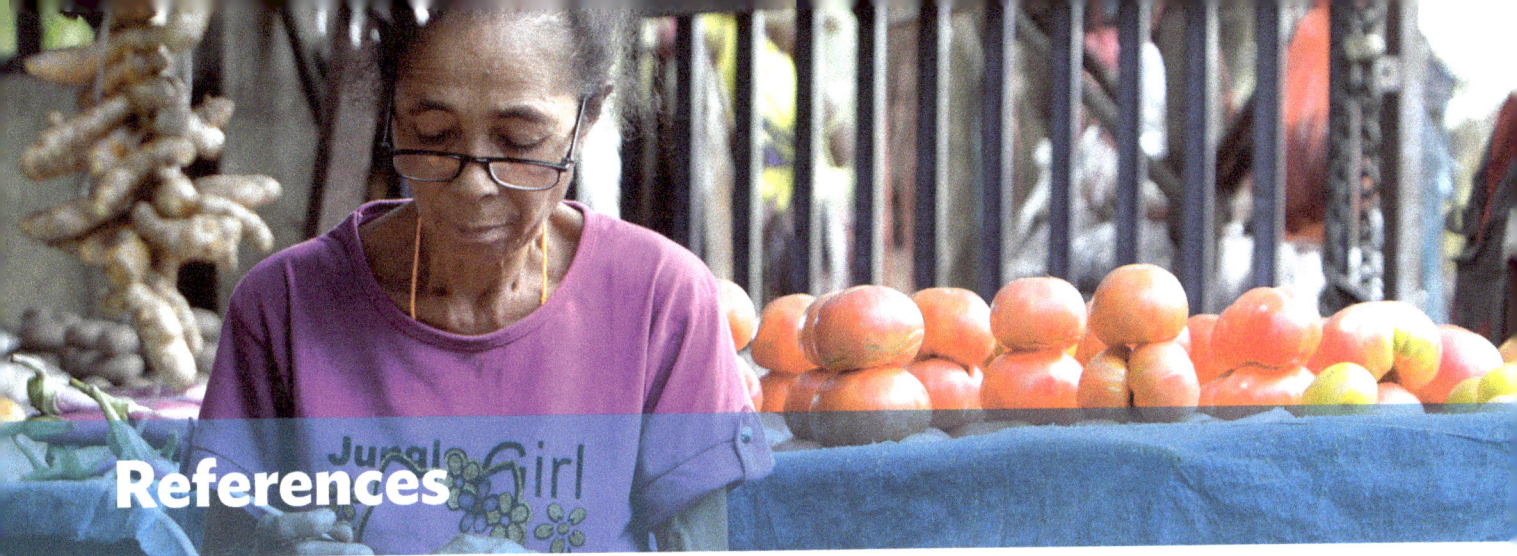

References

Brown, C., M. Ravallion, and D.V.D. Walle. 2016. A Poor Means Test? Econometric Targeting in Africa. Working Paper #7915. *World Bank Policy Research*. World Bank. Washington, DC.

Commitment to Equity. 2017. *CEQ Standard Indicators*. http://www.commitmentoequity.org/datacenter.

Demery, L. 2003. Analyzing the Incidence of Public Spending. In F. Bourguignon and L. A. Pereira da Silva, eds. *The Impact of Economic Policies on Poverty and Income Distribution: Evaluation Techniques and Tools*. World Bank and Oxford University Press. New York.

Enami, A. 2017. Measuring the Redistributive Impact of Taxes and Transfers in the Presence of Reranking. Chapter 3 in N. Lustig, ed. 2017.

Fullerton, D. and G. Metcalf. 2002. Tax Incidence. In A. Auerbach and M. Feldstein, eds. *Handbook of Public Economics 4*. Elsevier Science. Amsterdam. pp. 1787–1872.

Government of Timor-Leste, Ministry of Finance, Ministerial Cabinet. 2017. *State Budget 2017*. Dili, Timor-Leste. https://assets.ctfassets.net/60pzqxyjaaw g/5fiepJ3iJSqTQuxyglzM5U/06641d99832c00b1a6cd 4db9099d6552/BB1_2017_EN.pdf.

Jellema, J. and G. Inchauste. 2017. Constructing Consumable Income: Including the Direct and Indirect Effects of Indirect Taxes and Subsidies. Chapter 7 in N. Lustig, ed. 2017.

Lustig, N., ed. 2017. *CEQ Handbook: Estimating the Impact of Fiscal Policy on Inequality and Poverty*. Brookings Institution. Washington, DC.

Lustig, N. and S. Higgins. 2017. The CEQ Assessment: Measuring the Impact of Fiscal Policy on Inequality and Poverty. Chapter 1 in N. Lustig, ed. 2017. *CEQ Handbook: Estimating the Impact of Fiscal Policy on Inequality and Poverty*. Brookings Institution. Washington, DC.

PwC. 2014. *Timor-Leste Tax and Investment Guide*, 3rd edition. Jakarta, Indonesia. https://www.pwc.com/id/ en/publications/assets/timor-leste-guide-2014.pdf.

World Bank. 2016. Poverty in Timor-Leste 2014. World Bank, Washington, DC. https://documents1.worldbank. org/curated/en/577521475573958572/pdf/Poverty-in-Timor-Leste-2014.pdf.

World Bank. 2021. Timor-Leste Public Expenditure Review: Changing Course Towards Better and More Sustainable Spending. Washington, DC. https:// openknowledge.worldbank.org/bitstreams/6b16781d-b878-5a57-a851-f82909d131f6/download.